Teen Alcoholism

Look for these and other books in the Lucent
Overview Series:

Teen Alcoholism
Teen Drug Abuse
Teen Pregnancy
Teen Prostitution
Teen Sexuality
Teen Suicide
Teen Violence

Teen Alcoholism

by Hayley R. Mitchell

TEEN ISSUES

Library of Congress Cataloging-in-Publication Data

Mitchell, Hayley R., 1968–
    Teen alcoholism / by Hayley R. Mitchell.
        p.   cm. — (Lucent overview series)
    Includes bibliographical references and index.
    ISBN 1-56006-514-1
    1. Teenagers—Alcohol use—United States.   2. Alcoholism—
United States—Prevention   I. Title.   II. Series.
HV5135.M58   1998
362.29'2'0835—dc21   97-27500
                                                                            CIP

Copyright © 1998 by Lucent Books, Inc.
P.O. Box 289011, San Diego, CA 92198-9011
Printed in the U.S.A.

Contents

Introduction

ALCOHOL IS A DRUG. As such, it has the power to alter both the mind and body, and it is also potentially addictive. While most adults know the basic facts about alcohol and some of the inherent dangers of drinking, many of America's teens do not.

A 1996 report released by the Department of Health and Human Services suggests that most teens, for example, do not understand the concept of alcohol content and do not know the relative strengths of different alcoholic beverages. Fully 80 percent of teens do not know that a twelve-ounce can of beer has the same amount of alcohol as a shot of whiskey. A third of the teens surveyed also do not understand the intoxicating effects of alcohol.

Estimates show that at least 8 million American teenagers consume alcohol every week and that almost half a million go on weekly drinking binges, drinking for the sole purpose of getting drunk. Forty percent of tenth graders and nearly 20 percent of eighth graders, for example, reported having been drunk in 1996.

Education is key to preventing teen alcoholism

Perhaps if teens and preteens understood the effects of alcohol, the influences that lead to drinking, and the potential for social drinking to turn into alcoholism, many would not be the regular drinkers they are today. Perhaps if teens learned the skills for coping with emotional problems, the number one reason given by teens for their alco-

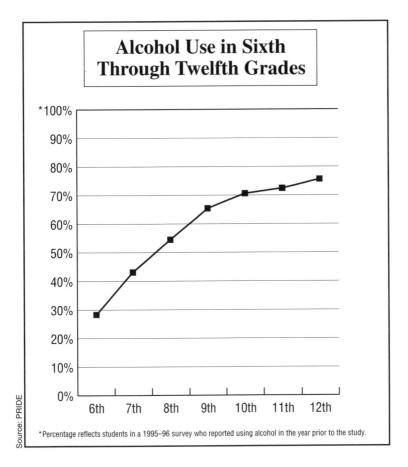

Alcohol Use in Sixth Through Twelfth Grades

*100%
90%
80%
70%
60%
50%
40%
30%
20%
10%
0%

6th   7th   8th   9th   10th   11th   12th

Source: PRIDE

*Percentage reflects students in a 1995–96 survey who reported using alcohol in the year prior to the study.

hol abuse, many would not take their first drinks before entering high school.

When teens drink, they not only put themselves at risk for abuse but also increase their chances of becoming involved in crimes, suicides, and violent encounters with others. They are also more likely to engage in risky sexual behavior. When they drink and drive, they risk adding to alcohol-related automobile fatality statistics. The number one killer of young people, alcohol-related traffic accidents, killed 2,222 sixteen- to twenty-year-olds in 1994.

While teen alcohol use in the United States is high, recent efforts are aimed at preventing numbers from rising even higher. From the kitchen table, to the classroom, to the local liquor store, new prevention strategies reach into virtually every aspect of teens' lives. Some estimates suggest

Young street kids spend the night drinking beer. Teens tend to drink to get drunk, without thinking of alcohol's potential addictive effects.

that more than fourteen hundred adolescents and young adults benefit daily from alcohol prevention programs.

More than 126,000 patients admitted to state-funded alcohol treatment programs in 1991 were under the age of twenty-one. In recognition of the fact that alcoholism is no longer just an adults' disease, numerous treatment programs now focus specifically on teen alcoholism. Though employing traditional alcoholism treatment methods, these teen programs focus on issues and problems that lead to teen alcohol abuse. They also give teens a chance to see that they are not alone in their problems or their struggles to get sober.

The special challenge is to educate teens about the potential dangers of drinking before experimentation with alcohol turns into alcohol abuse, and before abuse turns into teen alcoholism. Teens who may already be alcoholics also need facts about alcohol that can help them both determine and admit that they may have problems. After all, teen alcoholics are likely to become adult alcoholics whose children are likely to become alcoholics in turn. This cycle of alcoholism can be broken, however, when addicted teens are given the help and support they need to become sober, self-confident adults who are ready to become productive members of society.

1

Alcohol Is a Drug

ALCOHOLIC BEVERAGES ARE popular in our society, a so-called social lubricant at home or family gatherings as well as social settings such as parties or bars. When asked why they drink, people often respond that they enjoy the pleasant effects of alcohol. A shy person might say that drinking a few beers helps him to loosen up in large groups. Another person who works long hours might say that drinking a glass of wine with dinner helps her relax in the evening. Whatever their reasons for drinking alcoholic beverages, most people are aware that alcohol is a powerful substance that can affect both the mind and the body. It is alcohol's ability to alter body function, as well as its potential to cause addiction, that has led to its classification as a drug.

The toxic chemical responsible for affecting the bodies and minds of drinkers is ethyl alcohol (or alcohol). Ethyl alcohol is found in distilled liquor, wine, and beer. Beer contains the lowest percentage of alcohol at 4 to 5 percent; wine is usually 10 to 14 percent alcohol; and distilled or "hard liquor," like gin, scotch, and vodka, ranges from 40 to 70 percent alcohol. Although drinking large quantities of alcohol can cause a deadly alcohol poisoning, the toxicity of ethyl alcohol is more commonly known to cause intoxication, or drunkenness, just one of the short-term effects of alcohol.

Getting drunk

Intoxication is the result of drinking more alcohol than the body can burn off. This "burning off" process is called

The Amount of Alcohol in One Drink

 12 ounces of beer (5% alcohol)

 5 ounces of wine (12% alcohol)

 1.5 ounces of liquor (40% alcohol)

Each of the three types of alcohol listed above has about the same amount of ethyl alcohol—**.6 ounces**.

Source: National Clearinghouse for Alcohol and Drug Information

metabolism. When someone drinks, about 20 percent of the alcohol in their drink is absorbed directly through the mouth, throat, and stomach walls, and passes into the bloodstream.

Once dissolved in the bloodstream, most of the alcohol can be found in organs that require a large blood supply. One of these organs is the brain. When alcohol reaches the cells in the cortex, or outer layer of the brain, the way a person thinks and moves is altered. The drinker becomes drunk and may start to feel giddy and uncoordinated.

Although alcohol can make people feel giddy and give one the impression of feeling energetic, alcohol is, in fact, a depressant. Staggering and slurred speech occurs after drinking, for example, because the alcohol is depressing, or slowing down, the functions of the central nervous system, which includes the brain and spinal cord.

It is possible to measure how drunk a person is by testing blood alcohol content (BAC). The blood alcohol content is the percentage of alcohol found in the blood after drinking alcoholic beverages. If 1 part alcohol is found in 1,000 parts blood, the BAC is 0.10 percent.

Predicting blood alcohol levels is complex, however. The rate at which alcohol enters the bloodstream, and the speed at which alcohol reaches the brain, depends on several factors. For example, a large adult male would probably have a lower BAC after drinking one drink than a smaller, teenage female drinking the same amount of alcohol. In addition to gender and weight, BAC also varies depending on the amount of alcohol consumed, how fast a person drinks it, and whether there is food in the stomach at the time the alcohol is consumed.

When blood alcohol content rises

When BAC reaches 0.10 percent, speech may become slurred. At 0.15 percent, a drinker may stumble when walking. A person who continues to drink until BAC rises to 0.30 percent is likely to vomit as the body tries to rid itself of the alcohol, and may also become confused and disoriented. Finally, at BAC levels of 0.40 percent, the drinker often passes out. Since alcohol poisoning and death can occur between BAC levels of 0.40 and 0.70, passing out can be viewed as the body's defense mechanism in its attempt to prevent someone from continuing to drink.

There is no evidence that occasionally being drunk has long-term physical effects on the body. Considering that the body becomes uncoordinated as a response to rising blood alcohol levels, however, it is not surprising that one's chances of having an accident increase when drinking.

Studies of emergency room patient records and coroner's reports document high rates of alcohol involvement in fatal accidents. For instance, a 1991 study estimated that more than half the victims of fatal car crashes tested positive for alcohol use. In addition, approximately 35 percent of deaths due to falls, 43 percent of deaths due to burns, and 38 percent of drownings were alcohol related.

From euphoria to depression

When alcohol acts on the thought processes of the brain, it creates not only short-term physical effects but short-term emotional effects as well. As do the physical effects of intoxication, the emotional effects of drinking tend to last only as long as alcohol remains in the body.

The same depressant properties of alcohol that reduce activity in areas of the brain that control speech and motor skills also decrease the brain's control over behavior and emotions. The fact that alcohol consumption impairs judgment, reduces inhibition, and increases aggression explains why people often act on impulse or become overemotional when drinking.

"Sometimes alcohol can make you happy and sometimes it will make you sad," author Paul Dolmetsch writes. "When alcohol changes your emotions it can cause you to have abnormal responses to everyday goings-on. Maybe you will laugh at things that are usually not funny, or you will say things you wouldn't normally say, or maybe you will do things you have never done before."

A person's expectations, mood before drinking, and the setting in which drinking occurs all play a role in his or her emotional reaction to drinking. A person who expects to feel happy after drinking will probably experience that emotion. Likewise, someone who is depressed is likely to become more depressed.

Blood Alcohol Concentration Within One Hour

number of drinks

weight in pounds	1	2	3	4	5
100	.04	.09	.15	.20	.25
120	.03	.08	.12	.16	.21
140	.02	.06	.10	.14	.18
160	.02	.05	.09	.12	.15
180	.02	.05	.08	.10	.13
200	.01	.04	.07	.09	.12

0 to .04
Not legally under the influence. Impairment possible.

.05 to .09
State laws regarding BAC legal limits vary. Mental and physical impairment noticeable.

.10 and above
Presumed intoxicated in all 50 states.

Figures are rounded to nearest .01. BACs shown are approximate, since they can be affected by factors other than weight.

Source: National Clearinghouse for Alcohol and Drug Information

Two adults enjoy a glass of wine with dinner. Some experts believe that children who watch their parents use alcohol sensibly will be less likely to have negative emotional reactions to alcohol.

"If a person believes that drinking is a grave moral weakness and takes a drink, he or she is inviting immediate difficulties," cautions author Jane Claypool. However, she continues, "A person who is accustomed to seeing parents drink wine with meals may take the first glass of wine with no negative expectations." Alcohol is often used as a mood changer. In this case, Claypool says, it is important to remember that "instead of changing a mood, alcohol may simply deepen it." For example, an angry person who drinks to alleviate his anger may find himself becoming angrier.

Although emotional reactions can vary from person to person, because alcohol affects the area of the brain where self-control originates and learned behaviors are stored, there are a number of common responses associated with drinking. In general, after one drink, a person may feel more relaxed, might start to feel worries lifting, and may become less shy, to some degree depending on the drinker's

Young men and women drink beer at a local bar. Many young people drink to lose their inhibitions.

mood. In social settings, this initial relief of tension can lead easily to feelings of happiness or exhilaration.

After two to three drinks, people may feel less inhibited than usual, meaning they may do or say things they would normally censor. Drinkers at this stage tend to become loud and boisterous. In addition, their loss of inhibition may cause them to make or accept sexual advances they ordinarily would not.

A person who keeps drinking after the third drink is likely to continue to experience changing emotions. As the alcohol works its way through the bloodstream and impairs motor skills with increasing severity, the drinker may feel confused or frustrated by his or her lack of coordination. Some drinkers also become quarrelsome: People who have been told to "slow down" their alcohol intake because they are becoming drunk, or who have had their car keys taken away by concerned friends, may become aggressive and argumentative. The likelihood of verbal assaults and physical scuffles rises at this stage of drunkenness.

Researchers note that alcohol is not the sole cause of violent behavior, and that the majority of drinkers never engage in violent behavior. The U.S. Department of Health and Human Services reports, however, that in addition to influencing the perpetrators of violent crime, "alcohol is likely to be detected among victims of stabbings, among those killed in bars and restaurants, and among those killed on weekend nights," when the public's weekly alcohol consumption is at its peak.

Hangovers

When the immediate physical and emotional effects of intoxication wear off the day after a bout of drinking, drinkers often have to cope with another common short-term effect of alcohol: hangovers. Although there is no medical definition of a hangover, physical symptoms, which can differ from person to person, generally include one or more of the following: headache, nausea, dizziness, fatigue, and upset stomach. Emotional responses may include anxiety, depression, and irritability.

Hangover headaches, experts believe, are caused by an excess of fluid in the brain after drinking. Symptoms of fatigue correspond with a decline in blood sugar, and upset stomachs can be blamed on the disruption of the digestive system. People with hangovers often give themselves away by their bloodshot eyes, an additional symptom caused by alcohol-induced dilation of blood vessels.

Though symptoms vary, in general, a person with a hangover will simply feel unwell and unsociable until the body can return to its normal state. In their book *A Six-Pack and a Fake ID*, authors Daniel and Susan Cohen describe the hangover experience well: "You feel that you are being punished for your wickedness of the previous night," he writes, "and you swear you will never, never do it again. However, a hangover is not moral retribution. It is a purely physical reaction to more of that toxic substance called alcohol than the body can handle."

Surprisingly, hangovers are not always related to the number of drinks consumed. Experts agree that the severity of a drinker's hangovers increases with age, but beyond that, why one person may drink a single glass of champagne and feel very ill the next day and another person may consume many drinks and feel no negative effects in the morning is unclear. There are, incidentally, no known cures for hangovers. Friends may suggest taking aspirin and drinking black coffee to lift the spirits, but in actuality, time, waiting for the toxicity of the alcohol to wear off, is the only "cure."

Long-term physical effects

Hangovers are uncomfortable but not life threatening. There are a number of long-term, or chronic, changes that can occur in the body after prolonged alcohol use and abuse, however, that are much more serious. Like short-term effects, these chronic effects vary from person to person, but research shows that even so-called moderate drinking (that is, two drinks a day at most, for as little as a year) can have long-term medical consequences that can contribute to poor overall health, sleep disorders, and decreased fitness. Habitual drinkers are also at greater risk for developing chronic alcohol-related diseases, such as liver disease and some forms of cancer.

Although teens seldom have a history of drinking prolonged enough to experience many of the chronic alcohol-related diseases, alcohol does affect their health. Alcohol use by teens has been associated with cases of bulimia and anorexia nervosa, and has been proven to suppress the levels of growth hormones important for bone and muscle development. Adolescents who use alcohol have also been found to have increased levels of iron in the blood, which may be one precursor to liver damage.

Poor overall health

People who have engaged in prolonged heavy drinking often suffer a variety of ailments that contribute to poor overall health. In their book *Loosening the Grip*, authors Jean Kinney and Gwen Leaton explain, for example, that "chronic drinkers may complain of frequent belching, loss of appetite, alternating diarrhea and constipation, morning

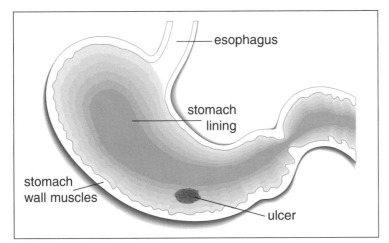

esophagus

stomach
lining

stomach
wall muscles

ulcer

A diagram of a stomach ulcer. Alcohol irritates the sensitive lining of the stomach and can cause ulcers or aggravate existing ulcers.

nausea, and vomiting." Frequent vomiting, they explain, can cause tears in the lining of the esophagus and may result in massive bleeding.

The potential for bleeding is also a concern for drinkers who have ulcers. Chronic alcohol use can both cause ulcers and aggravate existing ulcers in the stomach and small intestine. When bleeding occurs in these irritated areas in a heavy drinker (whose blood clots less rapidly than that of nondrinkers) the body's natural defenses alone may not be able to stop the internal bleeding, and surgery may be required.

Another common effect of chronic drinking is anemia. Alcohol is poisonous to the bone marrow cells that make red blood cells, and anemia results when too few red blood cells are produced by the body; many heavy drinkers feel the symptoms of anemia, weakness and fatigue.

Anemia is also caused by inadequate nutrition, common in heavy drinkers, who frequently have poor eating habits or digestive system problems that prevent them from getting the full nutrients they need from foods. Many people enjoy a glass of wine before dinner because they feel it promotes the digestive process, but though it is true that a single drink can "stimulate" the gastric juices and thus prepare the stomach for food, drinking more than one drink before eating a meal can impede the digestive process. When someone becomes intoxicated before eating, the alcohol can irritate the stomach lining and decrease the action of the digestive organs. If digestion is interrupted in this manner, it becomes difficult for the body to process the calories, or energy, it needs from food.

Heavy drinking can also limit a person's ability to participate in physical activities because alcohol interferes with the body's ability to absorb calcium needed for strong, healthy bones. In addition to potentially weakening bones, over time alcohol also weakens muscle fiber and irritates joints, making strenuous activities more difficult and dangerous. Chronic alcohol consumption reduces the production of proteins and prevents normal cell growth in muscle fibers. This process may lead to muscle pain, weakness, and eventually to muscle damage.

Sleep disorders

Chronic drinkers may also experience poor health due to alcohol-related sleep disturbances. Drinking alcohol before going to bed tends to decrease the amount of time one spends in the much-needed REM (rapid eye movement) phase of sleep, when dreaming occurs. Less time in REM sleep prevents one from experiencing a restful, deep sleep. As a result, someone who has been drinking may awaken many times in the night, and thus, never pass through all of the stages of sleep.

Chronic drinkers may experience this pattern of sleeplessness night after night, depriving the body of the restorative effects of sleep. Kinney and Leaton suggest that this "very poor sleep makes people want to sleep longer in the morning and during the day, which adds to the [alcoholic's] usual problems of coping."

Chronic alcohol-related diseases

The long-term effects of chronic drinking also include numerous alcohol-related diseases. Alcohol has been linked, for example, to heart, gland, and muscle diseases, and it can significantly increase the risk of cancer. Studies have shown a strong association, for instance, between alcohol use and cancers of the esophagus, pharynx, and mouth. Nearly 50 percent of these cancer cases in the

United States are associated with heavy drinking. As alcohol consumption increases, so does the risk of developing these and other types of cancers.

One of the most common effects of excessive alcohol intake is liver disease. The liver is the largest organ of the body and one of the most complicated, responsible for the production of bile, a secretion of glucose, proteins, vitamins, and fat. It also detoxifies numerous ingested substances in the body, including alcohol, nicotine, and other poisons. The three alcohol-induced liver diseases are fatty liver, alcoholic hepatitis, and cirrhosis, which a drinker may develop in any combination.

Promoted by heavy drinking, fat deposits may accumulate in the liver and interfere with its functioning. Evidence of fatty liver can be found in nearly all heavy drinkers. The painful liver inflammation of alcoholic hepatitis can be fatal; it is estimated that 10 to 35 percent of chronic drinkers develop alcoholic hepatitis.

The most advanced form of alcoholic liver injury is alcoholic cirrhosis. Cirrhosis is a term used for a number of chronic liver diseases in which normal cells are damaged by repeated inflammation and other disease-related processes. This condition is characterized by progressive development of scar tissue that chokes off blood vessels and distorts the size, shape, and function of the liver.

A liver affected by cirrhosis shows characteristic cell damage and fatty deposits from repeated scarring.

People with cirrhosis may develop kidney malfunctions, stomach ulcers, cancer of the liver, and serious bacterial infections; every year more than twenty-five thousand Americans die from cirrhosis. Steady drinkers are at a higher risk of developing alcoholic cirrhosis than binge drinkers (those who drink heavily but sporadically), and in general, patients with alcoholic cirrhosis have been drinking heavily for ten to twenty years.

Pancreatitis

Another common chronic disease related to heavy alcohol use is pancreatitis.

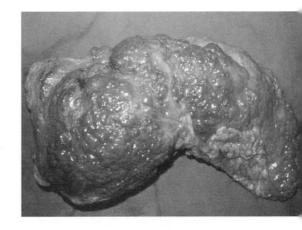

Long-term drinking can damage many of the body's internal organs. The esophagus (a), stomach (b), small intestine (c), and liver (d) are all subject to inflammation, bleeding, and other abnormalities.

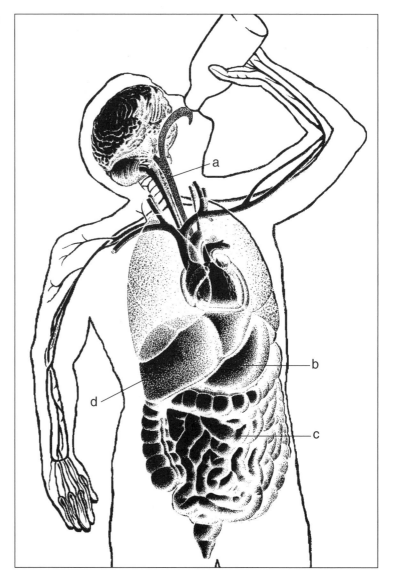

The pancreas is responsible for making digestive juices that break down starches, fats, and proteins in the body. Pancreatitis, an inflammation of the pancreas that can be caused by excessive drinking, prevents these digestive juices from passing through the small intestine. Symptoms of pancreatitis include nausea, vomiting, occasional diarrhea, and severe upper abdominal pain. As the disease progresses, recurring attacks of pain are more severe, more frequent, and of longer duration. Excessive and prolonged alcohol consumption accounts for 75 percent of all cases of pancreatitis in the United States. An alcoholic's chance of developing pancreatitis is fifty times greater than that of the nondrinking population.

Fetal alcohol syndrome

Although the health hazards associated with chronic heavy drinking pose the greatest threat to the drinkers, alcohol abuse can also directly affect the health of at least one other group. Women who abuse alcohol during pregnancy can inflict on their children a wide range of physical and mental birth defects, collectively referred to as fetal alcohol syndrome (FAS).

When alcohol is present in a pregnant woman's bloodstream, it circulates to the developing baby by crossing the placenta. There, the alcohol interferes with the ability of the fetus to receive sufficient oxygen and nutrients for normal cell development in the brain and other body organs. The symptoms of FAS include brain damage, heart and bone deformities, vision and hearing impairment, growth deficiency in both height and weight before and after birth, and facial abnormalities.

One of the most tragic results of alcoholism in pregnant women is fetal alcohol syndrome. Here, an adoptive mother holds her child who is affected by fetal alcohol syndrome.

Fetal alcohol syndrome is the leading cause of mental retardation. Although retardation has other causes, too, this one is entirely preventable. In simple terms, pregnant women who do not drink will not deliver babies with FAS. Researchers believe many cases of FAS go unreported each year, but based on reported cases, they estimate that of every one thousand live births yearly, one to three babies are born with FAS. In addition to the possibility of giving birth to children with FAS, women who are excessive drinkers are more likely than others to suffer miscarriages, premature deliveries, and stillbirths.

Alcohol-related birth defects and complications during pregnancy are not limited to heavy drinkers, however. Evidence suggests that pregnant women who drink as little as a drink or two a day have more miscarriages and deliver smaller babies who grow more slowly and have more behavioral difficulties than women who do not drink.

Alcoholism

One might wonder why some pregnant women drink despite the risk to the health of their unborn babies, or why someone who is suffering from poor health due to alcohol, or who is a candidate for an alcohol-related disease, continues to drink. In many cases, these individuals have lost all control over their drinking; they are alcoholics. They have become addicted to alcohol. Currently, nearly 14 million Americans (one in every thirteen adults) abuse alcohol or are alcoholic. Approximately 53 percent of men and women in the United States report that one or more of their close relatives has a drinking problem.

Alcoholism, also known as alcohol dependence syndrome, is a disease characterized by cravings, loss of control, physical dependence, and a need for more and more alcohol. Alcoholics crave alcohol in that they have a strong need, or compulsion, to drink. And, commonly, alcoholics share an inability to stop drinking. In other words, although alcoholics may be aware of the disruptive effects alcohol is having on their lives, their physical and emotional dependence on alcohol is so strong that they cannot give it up.

While some people who abuse alcohol may have an emotional dependence on the drug, alcoholics also have a physical dependence on alcohol. Physical dependence is characterized by the occurrence of withdrawal symptoms, such as nausea, sweating, shakiness, and anxiety, if alcohol use is suspended. Alcoholics relieve these symptoms by resuming drinking or by taking other sedative drugs.

Developing a tolerance to alcohol is also a sign of alcoholism. Building a tolerance to alcohol simply means that heavy drinkers eventually need more and more alcohol to feel its intoxicating effects. Roger E. Vogler, in his book *Teenagers & Alcohol: When Saying No Isn't Enough*, defines tolerance well. "If you drink every day," he says, "developing some long-term tolerance is inevitable. After a period of time, because two drinks no longer provide the high they once did, you may now have to consume three drinks to get the same effect that two drinks used to produce. After a while when three doesn't seem to do it, you move up to four drinks."

The "pre-alcoholic" phase

An increase in tolerance to alcohol usually develops in what Kinney and Leaton describe as the "pre-alcoholic"

People who develop a dependence on alcohol to "loosen up" in social situations are more likely to become alcoholics.

phase. Typically, during this phase, a person seeks out alcohol in social situations. Someone who is likely to become an alcoholic will begin to feel some kind of psychological relief from drinking in a social atmosphere. Psychological dependence may develop when this person begins to need to drink in order to do something, such as face a difficult task, loosen up sexually, have a good time, or unwind at the end of the day.

Soon the drinker may exhibit other warning signs of alcoholism. For instance, he or she may experience blackouts, or memory lapses, when drinking. The drinker may begin to drink alone before going out to parties, to gulp drinks, and to feel some guilt about his or her drinking.

The "crucial" and "chronic" phases

The next phase, or "crucial phase," is one in which drinkers tend to lose control of their drinking. Drinkers in this phase are "alternatively resentful, remorseful, and aggressive," Kinney and Leaton note. "Life has become alcohol centered. Family life and friendships deteriorate. The first alcohol-related hospitalization is likely." At this stage, the alcoholic has developed a physical dependence on alcohol. His or her body needs the neurochemical reaction produced by alcohol to function.

The final phase in the process of alcoholism is the "chronic phase," in which drinking begins earlier in the day and drunkenness is usually a daily state. In this phase the alcoholic may turn to drinking in places outside his or her peer group, such as bars outside the neighborhood. The alcoholic may notice a loss of tolerance to alcohol in this phase, and may develop tremors (shaking). Ultimately, Kinney and Leaton say alcoholics may be so determined to drink that they will drink anything containing alcohol, including rubbing alcohol.

2

Causes of Teen Drinking and Teen Alcoholism

To UNDERSTAND THE issue of teenage alcohol abuse, it is helpful to explore teen attitudes toward drinking and to discuss the issue of why teens drink in the first place. Social environment, peer influence, and, some experts argue, media influence contribute to teen drinking.

While these factors play a role in a teenager's taking his or her first drink, individual and family characteristics may direct a teen toward or away from alcohol dependence. A teen's personality and values, emotional state of mind, family lifestyle, and, possibly, predisposition, or tendency, toward alcoholism all may influence the descent into alcoholism.

Social environment

A national survey of 17,000 high school seniors found that alcohol was the drug most used in 1990. Ninety percent of respondents admitted that they had tried alcohol. Teen drinking is primarily a social activity; in fact, few teens report frequent drinking alone. The heavier a teen's drinking, the more likely it is to occur with peers. In 1995, for example, 40 percent of 270 teens in a national survey admitted that peers at their schools planned activities that revolved around alcohol and drugs on a weekly basis. Twenty percent admitted to planning drug- and alcohol-related activities on a daily basis.

Many teens use social situations as an excuse to get drunk.

During the high school years, teens are presented with numerous social opportunities. Weekly football games and other sporting events, parties, school dances, and class trips are just a few extracurricular activities that allow teens to socialize, relax, and have fun with their peers.

Although these activities can promote healthy social development, they may also provide opportunities for drinking and potential alcohol abuse. Sarah, for example, is one teen who began drinking with friends, first twice a month and then on weekends. She told author Roberta Myers that soon she and her friends, wondering, "Why wait all week?" began drinking during school hours.

Sarah explains that she was "just having fun"; she doesn't blame any "problems" for her drinking. By the time she was fifteen, Sarah was drinking until she "passed out most nights of the week," even when she was forced to drink alone. In addition to drinking alone, Sarah also kept beer under her bed so that she could "slam one before getting up to brush her teeth in the morning."

Drinking until passing out, drinking alone, and needing a drink to "get going" in the morning are all signs of alcohol dependence. Sarah, however, did not realize that her social drinking had turned to alcoholism.

Parties in people's homes are the number one source of alcohol for teens during the high school years. Most teens agree that planning a party with alcohol is fairly easy to do. Studies show that getting alcohol is not a problem for teens because minimum drinking age restrictions are not diligently enforced. For example, large numbers of teenagers purchase alcohol without legal proof of age: One source estimates that two-thirds of teens who drink—nearly 7 million teenagers—get alcohol simply by walking into liquor stores and supermarkets and buying it themselves. Other factors that make alcohol easy for teens to acquire are low retail prices and the willingness of some adults, such as older siblings, coworkers, and friends, to supply alcohol to teens. And whether or not a teen's parents are aware of it, their personal liquor supplies in the home are also a common source of alcohol for teens.

Peer influence

In the past, it was not uncommon for a teen to blame peer pressure for a drinking problem. But recent studies suggest parents overrate peer pressure as a factor in leading teens to drink. For example, the 1995 national survey showed that 87 percent of parents felt teens drink or use drugs because of peer pressure, or because "everybody is doing it"; in contrast, 79 percent of teens said they drank or used drugs because they "like the feeling of being drunk or high."

Today's teens may not be bullied or teased into drinking, but they are apt to follow their friends' leads. Researchers have found that peer *influence*, a more subtle form of peer pressure, can be a powerful predictor of alcohol use among teens. Studies show that the primary factors linking adolescent friends are age and gender, but the next most important are behaviors, including alcohol use.

Alcohol use often begins, or continues, when teens who have similar attitudes towards alcohol spend time together.

Teens interested in drinking are more likely to choose their friends among groups of people who also want to use alcohol and drugs. In the 1995 study, 40 percent of teens surveyed admitted that they had friends or classmates who both drank and used drugs. More specifically, best friends also play a role in predicting whether a teen may start drinking. One 1991 study found that teens were more likely to use alcohol if their best friend used alcohol or at least approved of drinking.

Media influence

In addition to peer influences, some experts believe that media depiction of alcohol use in print advertising, television and radio commercials, and fictional television programs such as sitcoms and dramatic series glamorizes alco-

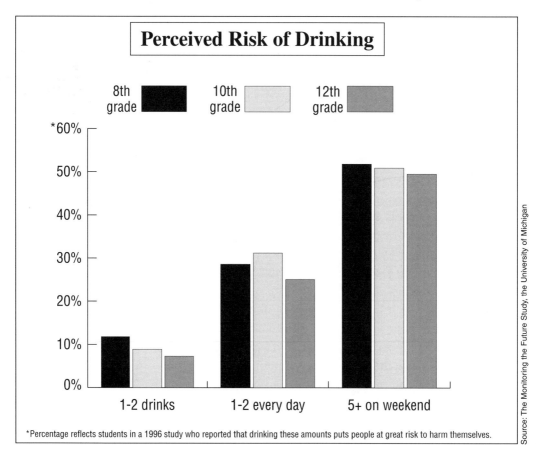

Perceived Risk of Drinking

8th grade   10th grade   12th grade

*Percentage reflects students in a 1996 study who reported that drinking these amounts puts people at great risk to harm themselves.

Source: The Monitoring the Future Study, the University of Michigan

hol to young people and can influence their decision to drink. Alcohol advertisers also promote their products in magazines, on billboards and posters, and on buses. Manufacturers of alcohol also sponsor prominent sporting events, such as the Super Bowl; radio contests; and rock concerts that are widely viewed by adults and young people.

Critics of alcohol advertising charge that advertisers are appealing to teenagers, that their promotional gimmicks not only reinforce the message that it is OK to drink, but in fact encourage underage drinking. Some alcohol advertisers employ professional athletes and actors who may be role models for teens as spokespeople, or link their product with handsome men and beautiful women in exotic settings.

The messages in these ads are clear: A person who drinks brand X will be sexy, win the game, impress the boss, etc. The ads attempt to show that drinking is fun, that it is cool, and that it will make a person popular. It is not clear, however, that these ads are aimed only at the legal drinking population. According to recent surveys by the *Wall Street Journal* and *Advertising Age*, many ads appear during television shows aimed at underage viewers.

Advertising bans

Critics of alcohol ads believe that they should be banned wherever they might influence the young. Research suggests that such bans do have an impact on alcohol consumption. For example, after studying alcohol advertising bans imposed in seventeen countries between 1970 and 1983, one researcher concluded that alcohol consumption in nations banning the advertising of spirits (hard or distilled liquor, such as scotch, vodka, and whiskey) was approximately 16 percent lower than in nations with no bans. Countries further banning beer and wine ads had 11 percent lower alcohol consumption than those prohibiting only the advertising of spirits.

In America, the liquor industry participated in a self-imposed television and radio ban of hard liquor advertising for forty-eight years. In June 1995, however, the voluntary ban was lifted after Seagram, a distiller of vodka and whiskey, bought air time on several television stations. The change in policy drew immediate criticism from lawmakers, who are now working on a bill that will formally ban many forms of alcohol advertising.

The new legislation would prohibit alcohol advertisements on television from 7 A.M. to 10 P.M. and require health warnings in the ads much like the warnings found on cigarette packaging. Advertisers would also be legally prohibited from creating ads that appeal to young viewers, of the sort for which beer manufacturer Anheuser-Busch has come under recent fire. In the targeted Anheuser-Busch ads, life-like frogs croak out the word "Bud - weis - er," a popular brand name. While the Budweiser frogs do not talk apart from their croaking out of the brand name, their actions are lively and exaggerated. The commercials are humorous and contain the kind of slapstick comedy often found in children's cartoons. In one of the ads, for example, a frog tries to catch up with a Budweiser truck as it rushes by the frogs sitting at the roadside. The frog unfurls its impossibly long tongue and attaches itself to the back of the speeding truck. The truck continues on with the frog flailing, seemingly happy, behind it. In response to this recent criticism,

Anheuser-Busch has pulled its advertising from MTV (a music cable television network aimed at young audiences), and plans to discontinue running its frog ads on all stations.

The distilled liquor industry has vowed to fight an advertising ban on its products. Aside from the fact that alcohol is legal for adult use, the industry contends that government studies do not prove a relationship between alcohol advertising and consumption. Advertising, in general, does not get people to buy products they would not normally use. Rather, it is aimed at getting consumers to buy a certain brand or type of product they already use or want to use. The same goes for alcohol advertising.

Advertising, industry representatives contend, does not cause an individual to begin drinking or to abuse alcohol any more than an ad for a particular brand of tuna fish influences a non–fish eater to buy tuna.

In response to the debate over teen drinking and advertising, President Clinton, backed by 240 organizations concerned about alcohol advertising, has urged the Federal Communications Commission to study the effects of radio and television advertising of all forms of alcoholic beverages on children.

Anheuser-Busch has been criticized for its hugely successful television commercial featuring frogs who ribbet out the words "Bud-weis-er" because it is believed the advertising appeals to teenagers.

Alcohol use in television programs

Alcohol educators are worried not only about the influence of alcohol in advertising; they are also concerned about how often alcohol use is portrayed in fictional programming, such as sitcoms and dramatic series, on television. As in the advertisements, alcohol use in television shows is often portrayed in a positive light. One 1990 study, for example, analyzed televised portrayals of alcohol in prime-time programming in the United States and found that nearly two-thirds of the episodes made reference to alcohol. Half of the episodes portrayed actual consumption, with an average of more than eight drinking acts per hour.

Like the glamorous and successful people in the alcohol ads, drinking characters in the television programs studied tended to be financially well-off with secure professional or managerial professions. Their alcohol use was portrayed as positive with almost no emphasis on the problems alcohol can cause. Researchers found that clear depiction of alcohol's negative effects occurred in only 10 percent of the episodes.

Some educational programs on television do warn against the dangers of drinking, such as *After School Specials* created for teens, and some ads do promote "sensible" drinking, such as the "Don't Drink and Drive" public service announcements generally sponsored by the alcohol industry. But critics, including President Clinton, claim that more needs to be done in this area to combat underage

drinking. Some say, for instance, that although the alcohol industry has done its part in anti–drinking and driving campaigns, its focus on drunk driving has allowed the industry to avoid the problems of chronic alcohol abuse.

Personality traits of teens at risk for alcohol abuse

Social environment, peer influence, and media influences may all play a role in a teen's deciding to drink, but external factors alone do not doom teens who drink to alcoholism. Experts have also identified various personality traits that can lead to a teen's abuse of alcohol. For instance, teens who are likely to abuse alcohol are prone to problem behaviors. Their personalities are often described as "sensation-seeking, impulsive, under-controlled, or thrill-seeking." These teens often experience problems with truancy and low grades. In general, they do not expect to succeed in school and do not strive for high levels of achievement.

Academic troubles are often one of the first indicators that a teen may be abusing alcohol, but problems in school are just the beginning. Teens who abuse alcohol are likely to become involved in other drug use, promiscuous sexual activity, and juvenile crime. In many cases, their behavioral and drinking problems stem from overeagerness to take on adult behaviors and rejection of authority figures such as parents, teachers, and police.

Emotional problems

Although teens with behavioral problems are very likely to be abusers of alcohol, one should not think that well-behaved, family-oriented teens who earn good grades are immune to becoming alcoholics. Even teens who do not cause trouble at home or school sometimes turn to alcohol for relief from the problems and stresses of their lives. One 1995 study, for instance, found that 66.7 percent of teens surveyed said that they use drugs and alcohol to help them forget their problems.

Problems that seem minor to adults often loom large in the emotional world of a teen. Moreover, apparently as a result of better nutrition, American youths now go through

These teenagers at Brooklyn Tech High School enjoy each other's company without the use of alcohol. The stress that accompanies high school and adolescence, however, can be a contributing factor to teen alcohol use.

puberty approximately two years earlier than they did a century ago. Thus, they are experiencing the stresses and confusions of puberty at an earlier stage of emotional development.

As youths go through puberty, body image becomes more important, and they worry about their hair, skin, clothes styles, and dating. Schoolwork may also be a source of stress for teens. High school workloads are heavier than those in middle school, pressure to study increases, and students may begin to worry about getting into college and deciding what they want to do with their lives after college. Added responsibilities that come with learning to drive or caring for younger siblings may also cause emotional problems for teens.

Certainly, some teen problems are much more serious than others. Some teens, for instance, may be concerned about, or in immediate danger from, gang violence in their neighborhoods. Others may feel pressure to have sex, may suffer from abusive relationships in or outside the home, or may be victims of bitter divorces.

Whatever the problem, teens who feel as though they have no one to turn to for help may turn to alcohol. Teens who drink to avoid pressures from friends, stress in the family, feelings that adults are constantly "on their case," or their own feelings of insecurity think that alcohol can make them feel better. This type of dependency on alcohol is an important indicator of alcoholism.

Once teens become dependent on alcohol they increasingly drink alone instead of with friends. When teens reach this stage they also drink greater quantities of alcohol than they would socially. In many cases this creates the additional stresses of lying to family and friends about their alcohol abuse. One fifteen-year-old named Brandy, for example, told author Sandy Fertman that she drank to loosen up because "it made me feel less worried about things. But actually, things only got worse," she said. "I worried a lot more."

Leah, a teen alcoholic

Leah is one of many teens whose emotional and family problems led her from social drinking with friends to alcoholism. Like Brandy, Leah thought that her drinking could fix her problems, but it only alienated her from family and caused her health to deteriorate. In 1993 she discussed her alcohol use with author Julie Monahan: Leah explained that she first got drunk when she was twelve years old. By her freshman year in high school, her drinking progressed to spending full days drinking with her friends in the park, chipping in to buy alcohol with her baby-sitting money. Eventually, she said, she did not see the point in drinking unless she was going to get drunk.

Leah's changing attitude about alcohol contributed to a loss of self-esteem when sober and irresponsible actions when drunk. She explains:

> When I wasn't wasted, I felt bored, lonely, and depressed. I thought I was ugly. I didn't fit in with anyone. When I drank, I felt more mature. I'd dress in revealing clothes and wear lots of makeup. Eventually, I got to the point where I didn't care what happened to me. Guys that I'd go out with would treat me really bad, and I'd let them. After a while, I couldn't have a good time unless I was wasted.

When Leah's parents divorced during her sophomore year of high school, she began drinking more frequently. She cut her classes more often and by the middle of the year was failing all her subjects. Left with few friends at school, Leah said she hated everyone. Like many teen alcoholics, she did not make it through the academic year. Students "labeled me a drunk," she said, and it "got harder and harder for me to go to school. Finally I just said forget it, and I dropped out."

After Leah dropped out of high school, she lost interest in just about everything except partying. She began to go out every night and drink and smoke marijuana with her friends. She would return home in the morning, sleep all day, and then go out and party again at night. By this time, her body was beginning to show many of the negative signs of excessive drinking. "I was underweight," she says, "and looked horrible. My face was this whitish yellow. My eyes were red all the time, and my hair was dirty. The whole summer I wore the same pair of jeans. I was like a junkie."

Despite signs of her physical deterioration, Leah was surprised and defensive when her mother suggested that she needed help for her alcohol abuse. She did not think that she had a problem. Drunks, to Leah, were "like old men who begged for quarters on the street. I thought, 'I'll never be like that.'" Soon, however, Leah did accept the fact that she needed help for her alcohol abuse and entered a group therapy program for teens. At the time of her interview, she had been completely sober for a full year, but she admitted that she will have to deal with her alcoholism for the rest of her life.

Family lifestyle

Upsets in the family and dysfunctional family life in general often add to the emotional problems of adolescents. Teens who feel that there is no communication or support within the family, or who live in families that are strained because of financial problems or because one parent is absent, may turn to alcohol for comfort. If one or both parents in the family also happen to be an alcoholic, experts believe

that teens may be predisposed (are increasingly susceptible) to becoming alcoholics themselves. Researchers in one 1990 study claimed that immediate relatives of alcoholics are approximately seven times more likely to develop alcoholism than the relatives of nonalcholics.

The predisposition to alcoholism has two theoretical explanations. The first is genetic. Genetic studies of twins and adopted babies indicate that alcoholism is to some extent hereditary. A kind of "gene for alcoholism," in other words, can be passed from parent to child, though the extent of this genetic influence is not known.

There is greater evidence, experts agree, that parental alcohol use and parental attitudes toward alcohol play a larger role in influencing teen drinking behavior than genetics. For example, parents who drink, either on occasion or abusively, tend to be more accepting of alcohol use in general than are abstinent parents. Some parents even allow their teens to drink at home on special family

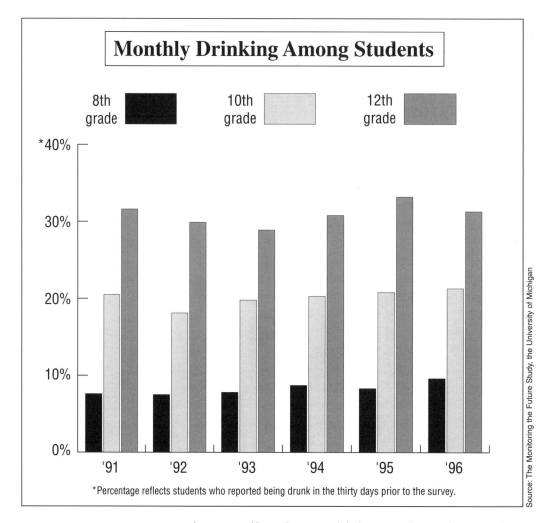

Monthly Drinking Among Students

8th grade

10th grade

12th grade

*40%

30%

20%

10%

0%

'91   '92   '93   '94   '95   '96

*Percentage reflects students who reported being drunk in the thirty days prior to the survey.

Source: The Monitoring the Future Study, the University of Michigan

occasions, or allow them to drink at parties as long as they promise not to drive home.

Parents are role models for their children. When parents drink at home, or express acceptance of drinking, some teens interpret these actions as permission to drink themselves. While it is true that some teens may turn to alcohol in rebellion against parents who strictly forbid teen drinking, in general, research proves that teenage alcohol use increases as parental approval increases.

One teen, Mark C., talked to author Paul Dolmetsch about his progressive alcoholism. His example demonstrates why experts warn parents and friends of teens against treating potential alcohol abuse as "just a stage" of normal adolescence. "In my earlier days, I would drink two six-packs a day," Mark says.

> By the end of my drinking I was drinking two fifths of whisky a day on the weekends plus four six packs each day. I got to the point where I would drink anything with alcohol. I had a friend whose parents made home brew in a crock pot. It used to be so strong that it blew the bottoms out of the bottles. We drank it anyway.

Certainly, in many cases family members may be unaware of a teen's excessive drinking until confronted by police officials, school authorities, or other sources outside the family. However, author Wendy Hamilton says, another key factor in continuing adolescent alcohol abuse is family denial:

> A 13-year-old may come home an hour late, appear quite lethargic, spend a portion of the night vomiting, and complain of a splitting headache the next morning. The parents may explain the behavior as a bad case of the flu. This easy explanation allows the family to avoid enormous family upset if the behavior is considered to be a reaction to alcohol abuse.

This type of family denial allows the teen to continue to use alcohol, and may encourage eventual abuse if the teen's drinking has not already become a problem.

In addition to their tolerance of alcohol use, parents who drink heavily have been found to employ less effective parenting techniques than parents who do not drink. One 1994 study, for example, reported that parents who drink heavily are less likely to monitor the behavior of their adolescent children and less likely to establish and enforce clear rules about drinking.

Any lack of monitoring, whether parents drink heavily or not at all, has a proven association with teens' joining peer groups that use alcohol or other drugs. In turn, these teens become more strongly influenced by their peers, and at an earlier age, than those who have had more parental guidance in their lives. Without parental involvement, guidance, and discipline, in an atmosphere of little family unity or affection, teens are especially vulnerable to developing drinking problems.

3

Problems Caused by Teen Drinking

ALCOHOL USE AND abuse can negatively affect a teen's health, put a strain on relationships with family and friends, and limit success in academics and employment. Teen alcohol use also plays a major role in teen crimes (such as theft, assault, and murder), teen suicides, and auto accidents.

In 1996 the Department of Health and Human Services reported that crime is a major consequence of youth drug and alcohol consumption. Nearly 40 percent of teens in correctional facilities, for example, reported drinking before committing a crime. More specifically, according to the Department of Justice, alcohol consumption is associated with over 27 percent of all murders, 31 percent of all rapes, 33 percent of all property offenses, and more than 37 percent of all robberies committed by young people. In addition to its association with teen crime against others, alcohol is often a factor in teen suicide. Each year 3.1 million adolescents (6 to 8 percent of all teens) attempt suicide, and drugs or alcohol factor into two-thirds of completed suicides.

Teen drunk driving

The disturbing relationship between teen drinking, crime, and suicide is topped only by the relationship between teen drinking and car accidents. According to the U.S. Department of Education, alcohol-related car accidents remain the leading cause of death among people fifteen to twenty-four years of age. Despite drinking-and-driving prevention programs, alcohol-related traffic fatalities (including both teen and adult drivers) increased by 4 percent in 1995, the first increase in ten years.

According to officials at the National Highway Traffic Safety Administration, alcohol was the leading cause of 41 percent of 1995's fatal automobile accidents. Jim Wright, who tracks teen fatalities for the administration, warns that any teen who drinks and drives is adding an extra element of risk to already hazardous driving habits. He tells author Pamela Warrick that "the normal teen-age driving pattern is often already impaired by poor judgment, inexperience, immaturity and dangerously divided attentions."

Teens need not be alcoholics to pose a threat to themselves or others when drinking and driving. Part of the teen drinking-and-driving problem can be attributed to the fact that many teens do not realize that even if their blood

A sixteen-year-old student died when his car hit a tree at 80 MPH, causing the vehicle to split in two. Alcohol is often the cause of such traffic fatalities.

alcohol levels are low, their ability to drive can be severely affected. In fact, the American Automobile Association reports that teens are at greater risk for fatal crashes than the adult population even after one drink. Drivers age 16 to 19 who have consumed 1 to 2 drinks, for example, are 7 times more likely to be killed in a crash than a sober driver of any age. After 3 to 4 drinks, they are 40 times more likely to be killed than a sober driver, and 20 times more likely to be killed than a 55-year-old driver with the same blood alcohol content. A teen who has consumed 4 to 6 drinks is 90 times more likely to die in a crash than a sober driver.

Despite publication of statistics like these, teens continue to drink and drive. Sometimes the effects of alcohol can make teens feel invincible, capably in control of their driving abilities. Some teens even mistakenly believe that their driving skills are enhanced after a few drinks. They do not realize that alcohol dulls the area of the brain that is crucial to decision making. Alcohol also decreases one's ability to concentrate, slows reaction time, and can cause blurred or double vision, all of which can contribute to a fatal drunk driving accident.

In most states, driving with a blood alcohol content (BAC) of 0.10 or more is against the law (some states have lowered the legal BAC levels to 0.08 or 0.05). Police officers have the right to stop suspected drunk drivers, who must submit to a BAC test. One way to test for blood alcohol is to draw blood, but a breathalyzer test (measuring alcohol levels through breath exhaled into a gauge) is given more frequently because its result is more immediate. Because it is illegal in most states to drink under the age of twenty-one, teens who are caught driving under the influence may receive license suspensions even if their blood alcohol level is under the adult legal limit.

The drunk driving case of James Patterson

Drinking and driving can have terrible consequences, not only for the person who drives drunk, but also for friends, relatives, and even absolute strangers. On July 29, 1995, seventeen-year-old James Patterson of Orange

County, California, discovered just how terrible the consequences of drinking and driving could be. Early that morning Patterson lost control of his father's truck while driving in the Mojave Desert in southern California. Patterson's four passengers—his friends Steven Bender, eighteen; Jonothan Croweagle Fabbro, sixteen; Tony Fuentes Jr., seventeen; and John Thorton, eighteen—were all killed. Patterson survived.

The events that culminated in the loss of four young lives began the previous evening. The five boys—including Patterson, their designated driver—had driven out to the desert for an evening of drinking. Over the course of the evening, a deputy district attorney said in court, Patterson had consumed at least ten beers. Although he stopped drinking earlier than his friends and tried to get some sleep before the drive home, Patterson's blood alcohol level registered 0.16—twice the legal limit for adults in California—when tested by police at the accident scene.

Patterson later pleaded guilty to four counts of vehicular manslaughter and two counts of felony drunk driving.

Young People, Drinking, and Driving

▶ Eight young people a day die in alcohol-related crashes. (CSAP, 1996)

▶ Younger people (ages 16–20) are most likely of any age group to use various strategies, when hosting a social occasion where alcohol is served, to try to prevent their guests from drinking and driving. (NHTSA, 1996)

▶ 7,738 intoxicated drivers (.10 BAC or greater) between the ages of 16 and 20 were fatally injured in 1995. (NHTSA, 1996)

▶ Between 1985 and 1995, the proportion of drivers 16 to 20 years of age who were involved in fatal crashes, and were intoxicated, dropped 47 percent, 23.9 percent in 1985 to 12.7 percent in 1994—the largest decrease of any age group during this time period. (NHTSA, 1996)

Source: MADD

A judge sentenced him to 120 days in jail and participation in an alcohol rehabilitation program, also for 120 days, a punishment some of the dead boys' parents believe was too lenient. Although Patterson acknowledges that his actions that night were all wrong, he also describes himself as an "average American teenager, doing average American teenager things, which frequently included beer." The lawyer who represented the families of the dead boys expressed concern about these remarks: Patterson, he believes, does not fully realize the connection between his own drinking and the death of his friends.

The drunk driving case of Daniel Blanton

The tragedy of drunk driving plays out daily across America, sometimes destroying the lives of people who are known to the driver—as in the case of James Patterson—and sometimes destroying the lives of complete strangers—as in the case of Daniel Blanton of Caweta County, Georgia. On December 20, 1995, seventeen-year-old Blanton's car collided with another car in Caweta County. Five people were killed in the crash, including seven-year-old Virginia Shaffer; her eight-year-old twin brothers, Daniel and Zachary Shaffer; the driver of the car, David Harris, age twenty-four; and his friend Dana Ogletree, age thirty-six and a father of five.

Blanton, the only survivor of the accident, admits that he drank three beers less than an hour before the crash. His blood alcohol content was measured at 0.08, the legal limit in the state of Georgia, and he also had traces of marijuana in his system. Although his exact speed has not been released to the press, police investigators also contend that Blanton was speeding when the accident occurred.

In July 1996, still in "disbelief" of the entire incident, Blanton pleaded guilty to five counts of first-degree vehicular homicide and one count of speeding. He was sentenced to ten years in prison. With good behavior he could be eligible for parole in three years. Kimberly Shaffer, the mother of the children killed in the crash and the fiancée of David Harris, was pregnant with their daughter at the time

of the crash. Disappointed by what she considered the leniency of Blanton's sentence, she expressed her shock that "a seventeen-year-old boy thought it was okay to smoke marijuana and have a few beers and drive a car."

The relationship between teenage drinking and sex

Another problematic and potentially dangerous aspect of teen drinking is its influence on sexual behaviors. Studies of teen drinkers show that they tend to consume more alcohol on a given occasion than adults. Teens also tend to get drunk more easily than adults because they are generally smaller and alcohol travels through a teenager's bloodstream more quickly. An additional behavioral effect that teens may not be aware of is that drinking even a small amount of alcohol can lower one's inhibitions. This means that even after one drink, teens may do things they normally would not, including participating in sexual activities.

One 1988 study performed by the University of California Task Force on AIDS in San Francisco questioned a group of fourteen- to nineteen-year-old girls about their attitudes concerning sex and alcohol. Seventy-one percent of these teens reported that they felt it was easier to have sex if they had been drinking. Another 1988 study found that teens who begin to use alcohol at least once a month are more likely than nondrinkers to have their first experiences with sexual intercourse within a year's time. The majority of teens who reported that they had not yet had sexual intercourse also reported that they had never used alcohol or other drugs, such as marijuana.

In a 1991 study published in the *International Journal of Addictions*, researchers conclude that alcohol can affect teen judgment in sex-related matters. The use of alcohol may influence not only teen decisions about whom to have sex with, but also the type, frequency, and duration of their sexual encounters. In other words, under the influence of alcohol, a teen who is ordinarily only comfortable with kissing may find himself or herself engaging in heavy petting or sexual intercourse.

A young woman brings her own six-pack of beer to a party. Young women are more likely to engage in sex when they have been drinking.

Risky sexual behaviors

Because alcohol consumption is likely to interfere with judgment and decision making, the chances of teen drinkers doing something "sexually risky" are also greater than normal. For instance, sexually active teens, most of whom already inconsistently follow safe-sex practices, such as using condoms, are even less likely to practice these precautions under the influence of alcohol. Studies have also found that those who had consumed five or more drinks in one sitting (known as binge drinking, and common at teen parties) were more likely than others to have had more than one sexual partner in the past year. Not using adequate protection, such as condoms, and having sex with multiple partners are behaviors that can result in unwanted pregnancies as well as sexually transmitted diseases, such as AIDS.

The *Journal of Substance Abuse* reported in 1991 that 58 percent of male teens and 48 percent of female teens surveyed had consumed alcohol immediately before their first experience of sexual intercourse. Only 13 percent of the drinking males used condoms during this first encounter. On the other hand, 57 percent of males who had *not* consumed alcohol before their first experience of intercourse said that they *had* used condoms.

In 1995, Census Bureau statistics showed that 13 percent of babies born in the United States were born to teen mothers. Approximately 1 million teens become pregnant each year. In addition to these high pregnancy rates, a fourth of all sexually transmitted disease diagnoses occur in teens. Experts believe that one way to curb these rising statistics is through educating teens about the effects of alcohol and its relationship to risky sexual behaviors.

Binge drinking

One behavior that contributes to sexual promiscuity and other problems at teen parties is binge drinking. Prevalent at teen parties, binge drinking is defined as rapid consumption of five or more drinks on a single occasion. According to the 1995 Monitoring the Future Study at the University of Michigan, 30 percent of high school seniors admit to binge drinking, an increase since 1994. Researchers who conducted a study published in *Public Health Reports* in 1993 raise some concerns about younger teens (ages fourteen to sixteen) present at parties where binge drinking is occurring. Older teens (ages seventeen to nineteen) told researchers that they would often "break in" younger teens by helping them to get very drunk, calling the experience "really cool."

Sara's ex-boyfriend is a binge drinker

One teen named Sara told author Jim Bernat that she was shocked when she first saw her usually shy boyfriend, Glenn, binge drinking at a party. "He was out on the porch downing beers with a couple of guys," she says. "I'd never seen him drink before. He was so loud and obnoxious. He sure wasn't acting shy anymore!"

That night, Sara watched as Glenn drank one beer after another. On a dare, he even drank a beer in fifteen seconds flat. When he was drinking, Glenn became a completely different person from the boy Sara had been dating. She says that he was "all hands" and acting rude to her in front of his friends. When Sara told him that she wanted to leave the party, he said, "No way! The party's just getting started. If you want to go, then go."

The next week at school when Sara confronted Glenn about his behavior at the party, he said that he did not remember doing or saying the things she claimed. He told her that he was sorry that he had had too much to drink, and he promised her, "It won't happen again." Glenn did not keep his promise, however. Sara recalls that at all the parties they attended together, Glenn could not stop drinking once he started. "He'd shotgun beers and do vodka chasers," she says. "It was as if the drinks at the parties were more important than the people who were there."

Glenn's behavior at parties is typical of binge drinkers and signals a serious problem with alcohol. Binge drinkers who have trouble stopping once they start drinking, who have personality changes when they are drinking, and who

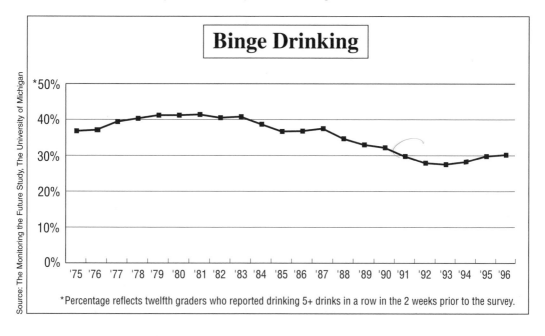

Source: The Monitoring the Future Study, The University of Michigan

Binge Drinking

*Percentage reflects twelfth graders who reported drinking 5+ drinks in a row in the 2 weeks prior to the survey.

cannot remember things that happened when they were drinking, may actually be alcoholics.

Glenn fits this description, but like many binge drinkers, he denies his problem. Glenn feels that since he only drinks at parties, and not every day, he is not an alcoholic, and he has everything under control. To Sara, though, it is clear that "his drinking is controlling him."

Binge drinking may lead to mishaps and violence

Young people imbibe large quantities of beer during a Memorial Day party. Binge drinkers use such celebrations as an excuse to drink to excess.

People, like Glenn, who deny their binge drinking problem often use alcohol as an excuse to act foolishly. In the morning, they can always say that they "don't remember." Students who binge drink at parties claim that they are not hurting anyone or that they are only having a good time. Studies show, however, that nearly all binge drinkers suffer some negative consequences of their drinking, though any later regret is usually not enough to keep binge drinkers from drinking in spite of problems.

One problem that can arise from binge drinking is violence. Binge drinkers often take risks and create dangerous situations for themselves and others when they are drunk. Writer Ed Carson, who studied binge drinking on college campuses, agrees that students get into trouble because they drink to have an excuse to be reckless. "'I was drunk,' is a get-out-of-jail-free card for college students who act like idiots, get into fights, or behave in other unacceptable or embarrassing ways," he says.

In general, college students, with increased opportunity to attend fraternity and sorority parties and other college social events, participate in the greatest amount of binge drinking. One 1991 study, for instance, found that 41 percent of the nation's college students (compared with 34 percent of noncollegiate drinkers) had engaged in binge drinking in the two weeks prior to the study. The same study predicted that in 1991 only 11 percent of the entire U.S. college student body would refrain from drinking. Another study suggested that unless something is done to curb student drinking on college campuses, as many students in America will die from alcohol-related causes as will receive graduate degrees.

Not everyone who frequently attends parties becomes a binge drinker, but teens can learn to recognize the signs of binge drinking in someone they know. In addition to the signs discussed above, if a person seems uncomfortable without alcohol at parties, and drinking and getting drunk becomes more important than friendly socializing, it is likely that he or she is a binge drinker. Concern for a person's drinking habits does not appear without reason, and the binge drinking problem should be taken seriously.

4

Prevention of
Teen Alcoholism

Despite the high rate of alcohol usage among teens, prevention programs throughout the United States are working to create significant changes in teen drinking behaviors. At the federal and state government levels, for example, new laws have been passed to enforce stiffer penalties for underage drinking offenses and drunk driving accidents involving teens. Local law enforcement officers in many communities have also supported prevention efforts by cracking down on establishments that sell alcohol to minors.

Statistics show that prevention also works at home and through educational efforts of schools and community-based programs that urge parents to talk to their teens about drinking. Numerous resources have been made available to parents to help them teach teens abstinence, or to help parents model "sensible drinking." In the schools, teens receive more information about the effects of drinking and alcohol abuse than ever before. Many schools even sponsor special "alcohol-free" events, such as dances and parties, to help teens have fun without the crutch of alcohol. And grassroots organizations such as MADD (Mothers Against Drunk Driving) work to keep the public informed about alcohol-related problems in their communities and are active in preventing teen drinking and, especially, teen drunk driving.

In June 1995, President Clinton urged every state in the nation to adopt a "zero tolerance" law that would penalize teens who drive after drinking. At the time of the president's speech, such laws were in effect in twenty-four states. Under the "zero tolerance" rule, anyone under twenty-one caught driving with a BAC of 0.02 (the equivalent of a single drink) or more must face the same consequences the states impose on adults considered legally drunk. In New York, for example, teen violators face a mandatory six-month suspension of their driver's licenses, a $125 fine, and a $100 fee to reinstate their licenses. Second offenders lose their licenses until age twenty-one.

Responding to the popularity of Clinton's "zero tolerance" campaign, lawmakers have continued to look for ways to curb teen drinking through legislation. In March 1997 the House of Representatives passed a nationwide

A sign advertises a "zero tolerance" program for minors. Many states have lowered the legal blood alcohol content for minors who drink and drive to .02 percent.

teen driving measure that is expected to come up for a vote in the Senate later in the year. Under the proposed law, all teens under eighteen who are eligible for driver's licenses will be issued restrictive licenses limiting the number of passengers allowed in the car and must abide by a 1 A.M. to 5 A.M. driving curfew. In addition, the new measure states that teens who are caught driving in excess of twenty-four miles an hour over the speed limit may have their licenses revoked. Lastly, the bill provides for mandatory twenty-four-hour jail terms for first-time teen drunk drivers.

Although drivers between the ages of fifteen and twenty make up only 7 percent of licensed drivers, they represent 14 percent of drivers involved in traffic fatalities. The main goal of restrictive licensing laws is to reduce crashes, injuries, and fatalities among these drivers. In December 1996, the Centers for Disease Control and Prevention (CDC) reported that teen drivers were involved in 7,993 fatal car accidents in 1995, a 23 percent drop from 10,415 teen-involved accidents in 1988. Government officials in such states as California, Florida, New York, and Wisconsin claim that this decline in teen car accidents is due in part to the various restrictive licensing statutes already in effect.

Sting operations

While lawmakers work to prevent teen drinking and drunk driving through state and federal legislation, local police departments work on prevention at the community level. Learning from teens themselves how easy it is to buy alcohol on their own, many local law enforcement agencies have focused on the outlets where teens purchase alcohol: liquor, grocery, and minimart, or convenience, stores.

In sting operations, police send minors (often underage, undercover police cadets) into retail establishments to buy alcoholic beverages. The teens are not allowed to lie about their age or show a false ID (that would constitute entrapment under the law), but in many cases store employees sell alcohol to them without even asking for ID. The object of these operations is to penalize merchants who essentially profit from teen drinking.

Such stings have had promising results in cities across the country. They appear to be most effective at preventing future sales to minors when they are set up two or three times a year. For example, in New York City, where manpower for enforcing underage liquor sales laws is limited, 90 percent of the merchants targeted for a one-time sting operation sold alcohol to minors. In cities where stings are conducted more than once a year, however, violations occurred in an average of only 20 percent of retailers. These numbers appear to show that the prospect of ongoing sting operations helps deter merchants from illegally selling alcohol to minors.

One offshoot of sting operations is a program called EASY (Eliminating Alcohol Sales to Youth). According to the *Addiction Letter*, EASY originated in Torrance, California, as a plan to educate local alcohol merchants, including servers in bars and restaurants, about ways to identify underage drinkers. Under EASY, a merchant caught selling alcohol to minors is given the choice of paying a fine or participating in an alcohol server training program. Retailers who are caught a second time pay fines and are warned that a third violation means arrest and the loss of their liquor licenses.

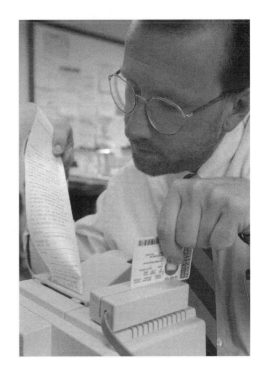

A demonstration of a machine scanning a driver's license to identify whether it has been altered in any way. Such scanners are used to identify underage drinkers who have tampered with the birth date on their licenses.

Reducing sales to minors

Inspired by the EASY program, a small town in New England implemented the sting program in 1994 and found to its dismay that 93 percent of its forty-one licensed alcohol retailers sold alcohol to the undercover cadet working the operation. In this case, all thirty-eight of the merchants in violation agreed to training for themselves and their employees. A few months later, a second sting caught only eight violators. There had been an 80 percent drop in sales to minors.

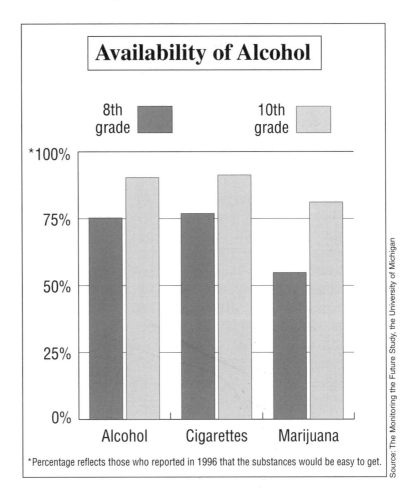

Availability of Alcohol

8th grade   10th grade

*100%

75%

50%

25%

0%

Alcohol   Cigarettes   Marijuana

*Percentage reflects those who reported in 1996 that the substances would be easy to get.

Source: The Monitoring the Future Study, the University of Michigan

Tony Guy was one sixteen-year-old who experienced sting operations from an unusual perspective. Guy worked as an undercover decoy for the vice squad in San Diego, California. His job, he said, was to buy alcohol in liquor stores, presenting his genuine ID when asked so that clerks knew they were selling to a minor. "I really looked, acted, and dressed like a typical sixteen-year-old," he says. Tony wore casual clothes in his role and says that he was not allowed to grow a beard or mustache. Female decoys in the program were also not allowed to take steps to look older; they could not, for example, wear makeup or jewelry. Each of the decoys also had to be willing to testify against offenders in court.

Tony explains that during the stings, retailers often looked at him in "disbelief," reminding him that he needed to be twenty-one to buy beer. When this happened, he said, an undercover agent would step in to explain the sting operation to the retailers and congratulate them for not selling to minors. On one occasion, however, Tony says that he was sold beer by an eight-year-old boy who was working the cash register for his mother. "His mother had to take the rap for him," he says, "because he was too young to be working in the first place, let alone in a liquor store!"

In the San Diego sting, retailers who were caught selling to minors could be ordered to pay $1,000 fines, serve six months in jail, or perform twenty-four to thirty-two hours of community service. Initially, Tony said, law enforcement officers had few guidelines to follow in operating the sting. By the end of 1994, however, additional guidelines to protect against entrapment and discrimination against stores in different districts were set up. The new guidelines required officials to notify stores in advance of sting operations and, on the day of the operations, announce the stings in the local newspaper. Even with this advance warning, Tony says, 20 to 30 percent of the stores he visited sold alcohol to him, but there was an obvious drop in illegal alcohol sales after each bust.

Prevention at home

While legislation has done much to try to curb teen drinking, experts suggest that alcohol prevention begins at home. Moreover, parents should not wait until their children are teenagers to discuss alcohol issues. Psychologist Kurt W. Jensen says that age seven is a good age to start talking to children about alcohol and drugs. "Children at this age," he says, "have some awareness of the subject, either from siblings, TV, or drug programs in the schools."

Professor of psychology Myrna Shure says that parents should try to find out how much their children already know about drugs and alcohol. For instance, they may not be able to discern the difference between drinking an alcoholic beverage at dinner and drinking to get drunk. Shure recommends that parents present kids with problem-solving questions about drinking. Ask them, for instance, how they think drinking would make them feel. Depending on their answers, parents could then ask their children what they could do instead of drinking that would make them feel "good," or what "would not make them feel sick."

The scope of these questions, Shure says, should show not only that alcohol is illegal for them, but that it can also be physically harmful. The benefit of this kind of dialogue between parents and children is that it allows children to come up with their own answers. As active participants, the "facts have more impact and children feel more competent." Most experts agree that public campaigns that urge young people to "just say no" to alcohol and drugs have little impact in preventing teen drinking, and that they need to learn the facts about alcohol at an earlier age. Shure concludes that children who understand why drinking is dangerous and how it can negatively affect themselves and others become much more resistant to the many influences to drink.

Talking to teens

Many parents assume that their teens already know that they do not approve of teen drinking, or that they cannot prevent their teens from drinking anyway. But experts stress that parents should let their teens know where they stand on alcohol-related issues. Studies have shown, for example, that teens who do not *hear* their parents say, "No," assume that their parents do not mind if they drink.

In a *Parent Talk Newsletter*, author Evelyn Peterson says that some parents feel telling their kids not to drink when they have alcohol at home is hypocritical. "Most kids have lived three fourths of their lives knowing that some things are off limits or for adults only," she says, so this attitude does not make sense. Teens, Peterson feels, need to be told by parents that "drinking under age is illegal, period." They need to be *told* not to drink, and *told* not to drive with someone who has been drinking.

Although the issue of whether parents should discuss "sensible drinking" with their teens instead of teaching abstinence is open to debate, many parents feel that this approach is more realistic for their teens; their strategy is to teach teens to act responsibly, which includes knowing the facts about alcohol and how drinking can affect them.

Someone who is drinking sensibly is presumably not drinking to get drunk. Author Roger Vogler offers tips for sensible drinking, including drinking slowly, eating while drinking, and avoiding drinking for more than an hour. Sensible drinkers do not consume one drink after another. Sensible drinkers do not, for example, drink to "ward off stress or a personal problem." Most importantly, sensible drinkers avoid doing things like driving or making important decisions when drinking. They also make sure that their daily lives are filled with more nondrinking activities than drinking ones. Lastly, sensible drinkers know how to refuse alcohol when they do not want a drink; they never let others force alcohol on them.

Prevention in the schools

Because teens spend most of their time in school, and not all parents discuss alcohol abuse or sensible drinking with their children, school settings have become a primary focus of alcohol prevention programming. Programs that focus on social influences, such as "peer resistance training," or attempts to change teens' faulty perceptions about alcohol use and its effects, have been most effective at changing drinking behaviors among teens.

Students Against Drunk Driving

One organization that has become influential in the schools is SADD (Students Against Drunk Driving). More than sixteen thousand chapters of SADD are active in schools across the country. Student members sign a contract in which they promise not to drink and drive. They also wear buttons and stickers encouraging other teens to do the same.

Members of SADD also participate in peer counseling sessions with teens who may be in trouble for alcohol abuse. Their involvement stretches beyond school grounds

Teens try out the Drunk Driving Simulator, a car that, with the help of an instructor using a laptop computer, can be used to simulate the braking and steering responses of a drunk driver.

as they try to raise public awareness and support for drunk driving prevention.

One preventive measure that SADD actively promotes is a signed agreement between teens and their parents concerning drinking and driving called the "Contract for Life Between Parent and Teenager." Under this contract, teens promise to call home (at any time and from any place) for transportation if they have been drinking. Parents agree to pick up their teens at any hour, or to provide money for a taxi ride home.

University prevention efforts

Once teens leave home and head off for college, drinking "contracts" with their parents can be full of holes. Traditionally, underage drinking at college, especially at fraternity and sorority parties, has been a popular pastime. In the past couple of years, however, many universities have taken steps to prevent teen drinking on campus. In September 1995, for example, fraternities at the University of Colorado voted to ban alcohol at their house parties. Other universities that have already set up bans or are being pressured to follow suit include Cornell University, Utah State University, the University of Washington, and the University of Iowa.

Colorado's ban came about, in part, as a result of the death of freshman Amanda MacDonald in March 1994. Returning home from a fraternity party, MacDonald was killed when the car in which she was a passenger went out of control and flipped over in the road. The driver had been drinking. The previous year, reporter Ben Gose writes, a "drunk Colorado student suffered brain damage after being punched in the face by a high school student and falling head-first to the ground" at a fraternity party.

After Colorado police authorities threatened to fine fraternities each time they caught underage drinkers at campus parties, fraternity officials decided that an all-out ban of alcohol was the only way to prevent teen drinking. Shortly after the ban took effect, fraternity leaders began to notice a change in the parties. One fraternity member reports, "It is amazing. The twenty-year-olds in the house are coming up to me and saying, 'This is incredible! We can have fun without drinking.'" In addition to curbing teen drinking, fraternities are saving money. "Alcohol budgets that averaged about $5,000 a semester," Gose says, "are now being used to hire better bands" and to sponsor unusual

A school official speaks with a student about his fraternity's decision to be alcohol-free. Notorious for their alcohol-binge parties, some fraternities are now trying to eliminate the image.

events like pig roasts. "It forces people to be creative," one fraternity member said.

Despite its apparent initial success, some University of Colorado students do not believe that the ban will last long. If the ban does last, students suspect that it will not stop teen drinking entirely: Students who are not allowed to drink on campus will simply find somewhere else to party. In this light, some Colorado residents are concerned that the ban will create problems in the university's surrounding communities. One student predicts, for example, that students "will drink in Denver or in the nearby mountains, and then drive home."

Community organizations

In addition to school-based activities, many communities have access to a variety of alcohol prevention programs. A unique program in Ann Arbor, Michigan, called Facing Alcohol Challenges Together (FACT), for example, works to scare kids away from alcohol and drugs. Reporter Brian Akre writes that participants, mostly youths referred by juvenile courts, along with their parents, tour local hospitals and morgues to receive a "heavy dose of reality" about the consequences of drug and alcohol use.

On one FACT tour, teens were shown the "effects of alcohol trauma" on human organs such as brains, hearts, and livers. Later, teens were zipped into body bags for a sensory shock. "The goal," program coordinator Dr. Paul Taheri says, "is to bring kids through the front door of the hospital now instead of through the emergency room later."

Possibly the most emotional moments of the FACT program are those involving teens' parents in role-playing scenarios with the hospital staff. Teens watch as a nurse tells their parents that they have died in an alcohol- or drug-related accident. They "hear the chaplain giving last rites to a pretend victim," and they "watch as hospital staff go over the bill with parents." For many teens, the shock of seeing their parents crying (more often than not, real tears) in the scenarios is enough to make them think twice about abusing drugs and alcohol. One twelve-year-old, Rachel,

says that she thinks the program can help teens resist some of the peer pressure they are feeling in her neighborhood.

Mothers Against Drunk Driving

More conventional in its methods and by far the most well known community-based organization is Mothers Against Drunk Driving (MADD). MADD was founded in 1980 by the mother of a thirteen-year-old girl killed by a drunk driver who had been released from jail two days earlier for another drunk driving accident. Since then, MADD has grown to include more than six hundred chapters nationwide. Members work to find solutions to the drunk driving problem and underage drinking, and offer a support network to families who have lost loved ones in drunk driving accidents.

MADD stresses its belief that people who drive drunk *choose* to do so. Therefore, MADD does not view injuries caused by drunk drivers as "accidents." Deaths and injuries

Relatives of victims of drunk drivers look over photographs on a MADD "victim board." Mothers Against Drunk Driving remains one of the most vocal and involved organizations dedicated to educating people about drinking and driving.

Senator Byron Dorgan of North Dakota speaks at a MADD press conference in Washington. MADD is an exceptionally organized special interest group that lobbies for stricter drunk driving legislation.

due to drunk driving, spokespeople argue, can be prevented. Although it is difficult to quantify the extent to which prevention-minded organizations like MADD have helped prevent drunk driving, fatality statistics have changed for the better over a ten-year period. For example, in 1995 there were 17,274 reported alcohol-related traffic fatalities in the United States. Although still high, this number represents a 24 percent drop from the 22,715 fatalities reported in 1985.

In 1995, MADD announced its goal to lower the number of alcohol-related traffic deaths by 20 percent each year until the year 2000. In addition to continuing to lobby for stricter penalties for adult drunk drivers, MADD has also been focusing on new measures to reduce teenage drunk driving. For example, MADD supports more stringent enforcement of minimum drinking age laws, and it supports Clinton's "zero tolerance" campaign and provisional licensing programs. MADD also calls for legal sanctions against people who make fake ID cards for teens, and for teens who seek these illegal IDs to buy alcohol. Parents, or other adults who knowingly provide alcohol to minors, MADD believes, should also be punished by law.

Teen SafeRides

Similar to SADD and MADD, another community-based organization that has worked for the prevention of teen drunk driving is Teen SafeRides. This group generally operates on Friday and Saturday nights, between the hours of 11 P.M. and 3 A.M., offering the volunteer services of sober teen drivers to teens who are unable to drive home safely. Whether teens have been stranded at parties by others who are too drunk to drive, or have been drinking themselves, SafeRides offers to get teens home confidentially and free of charge.

Communities that offer SafeRides programs or others like them generally list them in the Community Services sections of local phone books. While SafeRides organizers insist that they do not condone teen drinking, they encourage teens to keep their number handy when attending parties or other social events where there may be drinking.

Through the efforts of organizations like SADD, MADD, and Teen SafeRides, students and the general public have become more aware of the scope and tragic consequences of drunk driving. In response, some schools and community social groups now sponsor alcohol-free graduation celebrations, travel opportunities, and other social events for teens.

5

Treatment and Recovery

DESPITE THE EFFORTS of law enforcement, families, and school- and community-based programs, alcoholism prevention does not always work. Alcoholism, however, is treatable, and the sooner a person is able to acknowledge a need for help, the better are his or her chances for recovery. The types of programs suitable for alcoholics vary. The severity of an individual's drinking problem and available community resources, for example, are factors to be considered when choosing rehabilitation programs.

Some alcoholics seek treatment in hospital or residential-care settings. In these cases, they move into the facilities until they can get their drinking under control. Other alcoholics may select treatment on an outpatient basis: This choice is most appropriate for patients who do not want to interrupt their daily work or living arrangements. In both options, treatment may include detoxification, which is the process of slowly and safely getting alcohol out of the patient's system; prescribed medications, which help prevent patients from returning to drinking after they have stopped; and individual or group counseling.

Medications and counseling

When alcoholics first seek treatment after periods of heavy, continuous drinking, there is a strong likelihood that they will suffer withdrawal symptoms, including seizures and hallucinations. These symptoms generally last

This young man can already call himself "a recovering alcoholic." He attends Alcoholics Anonymous meetings daily to give him the support and fortitude to continue to avoid alcohol.

from five to eight days, and they can be treated with medication in a hospital or clinic.

In addition to receiving drugs for withdrawal management, patients may later be prescribed medications, such as anticraving agents, that decrease the desire for alcohol consumption. Other medications can be taken that provoke negative physical reactions, such as vomiting, when alcohol is ingested, reinforcing a patient's willingness not to drink. Finally, drugs are also available that reverse the intoxicating effects of alcohol. Should an alcoholic who is on these drugs decide to drink, he or she would be unable to get drunk.

Although alcoholism is treatable, there is no guarantee that an alcoholic will stop drinking. After they have regained health through medical treatment, alcoholics must make an effort every day to remain sober. The prevailing opinion is that alcoholics cannot just cut down on their drinking. They must avoid all alcoholic beverages if they are to achieve complete, long-term sobriety. On the road to sobriety, relapses, brief or extended periods of drinking, are very common.

To help prevent relapses, health professionals recommend alcoholics join "aftercare" counseling programs as part of their treatment. There are a number of counseling groups available to alcoholics that help alcoholics commit to a lifetime of sobriety. These groups include confidential self-help organizations that offer assistance to anyone who has a drinking problem and wants to deal with it.

In counseling, alcoholics are taught how to identify feelings and situations in their lives that may lead them to drink. They are encouraged to find new, positive ways of dealing with these situations that do not include drinking alcohol. There is generally no fee for the services of these counseling organizations. In addition, meetings are held in most communities, and friends and family members are often encouraged to attend.

Alcoholics Anonymous

One of the most widely adapted aftercare programs is Alcoholics Anonymous (AA). AA is a so-called twelve-step, mutual help program that stresses spiritual growth. As a first step, all members of AA are asked to admit that they are alcoholics who cannot manage their own lives. They recognize that "no human power could have relieved" their alcoholism. In this light, many of the twelve steps dictate that members place their faith in God in order to reach full recovery. Step three, for example, involves making "a decision to turn our will and our lives over to the care of God as we understand him."

Studies show that belief in the twelve-step philosophy of AA, not necessarily the number of meetings attended, is important to the recovery process. Another important aspect of AA is sponsorship. In AA, longtime members "sponsor" newer members to help them reach sobriety. Studies show that such sponsorship has a strong impact on sobriety. For example, 91 percent of AA sponsors report complete or stable remission of alcoholism.

Sobriety High, a special program for teens

Although teen alcoholism treatment programs include the same treatment options as adult programs, many teens prefer these programs because they can recover from their addictions with others their age. Like adult programs, teen treatment centers encourage the development of peer resistance, social skills, and relapse-prevention techniques.

There are numerous traditional, teen-oriented treatment centers, as well as some programs in less traditional settings, throughout the United States. One special program, for example, is Sobriety High, in Edina, Minnesota, where, Roberta Myers writes, "staying off drugs and alcohol is not only cool but a graduation requirement." Up to forty-three students can attend Sobriety High, instead of their regular high schools, at one time. They must be diagnosed as chemically dependent, and they must have completed drug- or alcohol-addiction programs before they can be admitted. In addition, students must sign a contract, pledging to remain sober.

Unlike traditional high schools, Sobriety High students graduate in six, not four, years. Sobriety High also assigns no homework. Instead, students spend their afterschool time working through their addictions. They meet with school counselors, for example, and many also attend AA meetings or other counseling groups. Despite the no-homework policy, students who graduate from Sobriety

'All bottles seem to be labelled "Drink Me".'

High receive the same level of education as other public schools in Minnesota. The state board of education sets curriculum, and grades, Myers writes, are based on "attendance, participation, in-class assignments, and tests."

Sobriety High founder Ralph Neiditch believes that the school is a haven for alcohol- and drug-addicted teens. The "worst place for kids with drug problems," he says, "is high school, where drinking and getting high are so common." At Sobriety High, these teens not only escape the drug environments of their schools and neighborhoods, they also learn respect for themselves and others. One sixteen-year-old, Jay, says, "They really care about you here. They listen to your problems and don't just say 'We'll get over it.'"

Sobriety High not only teaches respect, but also forces teens to take a serious look at the effects of their addictions. Sixteen-year-old student Sarah Smith, who began drinking heavily at age eleven, says that Sobriety High helped her to "confront the shame she felt about using, about being used, and about how much she hurt her mom."

Two students from Sobriety High in Edina, Minnesota.

She says, "If I weren't sober I could be pregnant, I could be kicked out of my house—who knows where I'd be?" In 1995 Sarah was beginning to look forward to graduating and attending college. She says that she'll accept her diploma with pride. "That diploma stands for a lot," she says. "It says I'm sober," and, she adds, "I've accomplished something. Something a hell of a lot harder than most people ever will."

Sobriety in college dorms

Minnesota is not the only state to recognize that it is sometimes difficult for teens recovering from drug and alcohol abuse to remain sober while in a school setting. Many universities, for example, offer drug- and alcohol-free dormitories. Rutgers University in New Jersey, however, is the only university that offers special "recovery housing" for students who are trying to overcome drinking problems. At Rutgers, the recovery housing helps up to twenty-five students remain sober while living on campus. These students want to "live on campus and be a part of the campus community," reporter Drake Witham writes, "but they don't want to live in residence halls, where many social activities center on alcohol."

The location of the Rutgers recovery housing is kept secret to protect the identity of its occupants, but otherwise it is similar to other college dorms. Students become close to one another, and often spend much of their weekends and free time together. Unlike other dorms, however, where some "rules" may frequently be bent or broken, the recovery dorms take their sobriety rules very seriously. Not only are students not allowed to drink or use drugs themselves, they are also not allowed to bring anyone who is "drunk or stoned" into the dorms. Director and counselor Lisa Laitman says, "We're looking for people who want to stay sober, not just those who want to appease their parents."

Alcoholism treatment decreases crime

Helping alcoholics gain control of their addictions is beneficial to everyone, not just alcoholics. Each year, alcohol-related crimes cost the country billions of dollars. Alcohol treatment programs help lower alcohol-related crime rates, thus saving taxpayers money. The health care industry and employers also reap the benefits of substance abuse treatment programs.

In 1994 the results of California's largest drug and alcohol treatment assessment were released. The study, called CALDATA, surveyed three thousand providers and participants in treatment programs from October 1991 through September 1992. The CALDATA study found a decrease in criminal activity among people who successfully completed treatment programs. Following treatment, the report states, the "level of crime declined by two-thirds" in cities participating in the study. The results of the California study are mirrored in studies across the nation. One fourteen-state study, for example, found that 79 percent of patients who received drug and alcohol abuse treatment and remained sober had not been arrested for criminal activity one year after treatment. Those who resumed drinking, however, had a 31 percent arrest rate.

Health and economic benefits

In addition to contributing to crime reduction, substance abuse programs also save money in the nation's health care industry. Health care experts estimate that alcoholics and drug addicts require medical services twenty times more often than nonaddicts. Untreated alcoholics, in particular, incur 100 percent more health care costs than nonalcoholics. With treatment programs in place, however, the California study estimates one-third reductions in both alcohol-related emergency room admissions and hospitalizations. A similar study in Minnesota found that by providing substance abuse programs, the state saves $22 million annually in health care costs.

Lastly, the American economy also benefits from substance abuse programs. Employees who are alcoholics or drug addicts are absent from work more often than nonabusers because they have more illnesses and injuries. Their absenteeism decreases productivity and also drives up costs in medical and disability claims. According to a 1992 Rutgers University study, under these conditions, untreated addictions cost American businesses from $50 to $100 billion each year. Treatment programs, however, reduce the number of sick days and medical claims by more than 50 percent.

Support system of family and friends

Given that society benefits from alcoholism treatment programs, those who reap the most rewards from sobriety are the alcoholics themselves. To achieve full recovery, however, alcoholics need the support of their loved ones. Family involvement, for instance, is important for an alcoholic's recovery. In fact, many treatment centers offer family counseling to their patients.

One of the ways that family and friends can aid an alcoholic's recovery is to learn what to expect during recovery. Recovery usually occurs in three stages. The first stage

Alcoholism does not just affect teenagers. Here, a homeless alcoholic man avails himself of a detox shelter to try to gain control of his alcohol problem.

focuses on getting well, write Arlene and Howard Eisenberg and Al J. Mooney. At this stage, the alcoholic is dependent on sobriety for physical survival. In the second stage, after sobriety is reached, alcoholics work on "rebuilding relationships, reevaluating career goals, and getting back into recreational activities." Finally, in the last stage of recovery, alcoholics achieve a "solid recovery lifestyle" by practicing better eating habits, establishing regular exercise routines, and cutting back on aftercare programs.

The first stage of recovery generally lasts a year or more. During this first stage, family relationships may become strained as family members learn how to live with a newly sober person. In families in which alcohol abuse has been an issue for an extended period of time, the sober alcoholic may seem like a stranger. Experts warn that alcoholics in this stage of recovery will suffer from dramatic mood swings. They may also seem to lack direction in their lives at school, work, or in the social realm.

Loved ones are generally disappointed during the first stage of recovery that the alcoholic's new sobriety has not magically cleared up any unresolved problems or past resentments. In their attempt to get sober, however, alcoholics have little time or energy in this phase to work through past problems. Rather than pushing communication issues, family and friends can be supportive during this phase simply by spending time with the alcoholic. Fun activities should be planned, such as going on walks, going to the movies, or just relaxing, talking, and enjoying each other's company. Family and friends should also plan on attending numerous aftercare meetings with the alcoholic.

Working out problems

The second stage of recovery, which can also last up to a year or more, is the best time to address problems in family or personal relationships. If alcoholics have not sought professional therapy before this time, they are encouraged to do so. In this stage, the alcoholic and his or her family and friends need to learn how to communicate their feelings without anger. It is important during this stage for

everyone involved in the recovery process to be thoughtful, forgiving, and open with each other, and controlling behavior is discouraged.

Experts suggest that stage two is the best time to discuss issues of denial or family conflict that have been previously ignored, to break patterns that might otherwise repeat themselves in the next generation.

A meeting of adult children of alcoholics ends in a group hug. Children of alcoholics tend to share similar problems in adulthood and use the group for support and reassurance.

Developing a new lifestyle

In the third stage of recovery, it is extremely important that all household members help the recovering alcoholic maintain a new, healthy lifestyle. The requirements of this stage are for the recovering alcoholic to make conscious efforts to eat healthy foods, exercise regularly, and quit smoking. This last requirement helps prevent an alcoholic from replacing their alcohol addiction with an increase in smoking. Finally, loved ones should remain supportive of an alcoholic's desire to continue attending AA or other aftercare programs as needed. Most alcoholics have a greater

A recovering alcoholic teen (far left) and her mother are interviewed for a talk show. Parents may be uncomfortable with a child's drinking problem, but their love and support is vital to the alcoholic's recovery.

chance of maintaining their sobriety if they do not drop out of these programs completely.

Though the three stages of recovery are common to most recovering alcoholics, alcoholism treatment experts stress that family members should not feel that they can map a loved one's recovery. Alcoholics need to be able to work through their recovery programs at their own pace.

The more parents, friends, and educators know about teen attitudes towards drinking and the progression of teen alcoholism, the better. Although admitting a teen member of the family has a problem with alcohol is difficult because parents and siblings may be experiencing feelings of fear and guilt, once these feelings are set aside, family members are better able to guide teens towards treatment, recovery, and a clean and sober lifestyle.

Physicians warn that while their support is important, it is not the job of family and friends to get recovering alcoholics, of any age, to meetings or counseling sessions. They should not feel as though they have to check for alcohol on the alcoholic's breath or examine their rooms for signs of alcohol abuse. Many alcoholics may not even have the benefit of support from family and friends. If they are to recover fully, alcoholics must be ready to take full responsibility for their own sobriety.

Teen alcoholic Leah suggests that taking that responsibility is not always easy, but to her, it has been worth the effort. She explains, for example, that she misses drinking every day of her sobriety. "But whenever I feel that way," she says, "I read my old diary, which makes me want to cry because my life was so empty [when I was drinking]. I had no goals, no friends, no real boyfriends." While in treatment, Leah learned to gain a positive attitude about life. She went back to high school and began to make plans for college.

Hope for the future

Leah's success story, and the stories of many teens like her who have fought their alcoholism and have taken control of their lives, can give hope to other teens who feel that they will never win in the battle over their addiction. Some teen alcoholics, however, may deny or not even be aware of their own alcoholism; others may not know that treatment is available to them should they want it; and still others may simply not be ready to give up their dependence on alcohol.

Society cannot force existing teen alcoholics to confront their problems, and in the United States, where alcohol remains the most widely abused drug, it may be impossible to prevent some teens from becoming alcoholics. Society can, however, continue to educate teens through alcohol prevention programs. Parents, teachers, and community leaders can also take steps to educate themselves about current teen attitudes towards drinking, and they can strive to offer alternatives as well as emphasize the responsibilities of sensible drinking.

Appendix

Common Signs of Teen Alcohol Abuse

- Missing classes, or a sudden drop in grades
- Drinking alcohol on school grounds
- Dropping old friends and changing peer groups
- Not bringing friends home after school
- Dressing differently, lack of grooming
- Decreased interest in family, social activities, sports, or hobbies
- Other family members who abuse alcohol (genetic predisposition)
- Drinking alone
- Drinking until the bottle is empty
- Having trouble stopping drinking once started
- Often drinking five drinks or more on a single occasion
- Feeling guilty after drinking
- Saying things one later regrets
- Taking risks or doing dangerous things when drinking
- Frequent accidents as a result of drinking
- Not remembering things that happened while drinking
- Being uncomfortable without alcohol
- Drinking becomes more important than anything else
- Legal difficulties, such as being arrested for drinking-related behavior
- Continuing to drink even after drinking episodes have caused problems
- Possessing fake identification

- Physical changes, such as memory lapses, slurred speech, loss of motor coordination, bloodshot eyes, dilated pupils
- Excessive use of eyedrops
- Frequent "flu" episodes, such as chronic cough, chest pains, and allergy symptoms
- Mood swings, such as irritability and hostility
- Verbal or physical abuse of younger siblings
- Feelings of loneliness, paranoia, and depression
- Drinking to relieve feelings of shyness and to build up self-confidence
- Expressed concern from others about drinking

Glossary

abstinence: Choosing not to participate in a behavior, such as drinking, on all occasions.

abuse: The misuse or overuse of a substance.

acquired immunodeficiency syndrome (AIDS): An incurable and fatal disease of the body's immune system; the viral agent, HIV, can be sexually transmitted.

addiction: Having a physical or psychological dependence on a substance.

Alcoholics Anonymous: A self-help support program for alcoholics that includes meetings that follow the twelve-step recovery plan.

alcoholism: A chronic condition caused by uncontrollable and habitual excessive drinking of alcohol, in which a person has become addicted to alcohol.

anemia: A medical condition in which a person's blood does not carry a normal amount of oxygen; one of the main symptoms is fatigue.

anorexia nervosa: An eating disorder marked by loss of appetite and extreme, dangerous weight loss.

anxiety: A painful or apprehensive uneasiness of mind; self-doubt about one's ability to cope.

binge drinking: Often a signal of alcoholism; drinking five or more drinks on a single occasion.

blackout: A memory lapse while drinking; very common among alcoholics.

blood alcohol content (BAC): The percentage of alcohol in a person's bloodstream.

breathalyzer: A device used by law enforcement officers to measure the blood alcohol content of a person suspected of drunk driving.

bulimia: An eating disorder marked by extreme cravings for food; large amounts of food are ingested but then "purged" from the system through vomiting.

chronic: Any condition which recurs or continues for long periods of time.

cirrhosis: A disease in which liver tissue becomes scarred and damaged by alcohol abuse and can no longer process the nutrients in food.

depressant: A substance that slows down mental and bodily functions.

depression: A state of feeling sad, generally for extended periods of time.

detoxification: Elimination of drugs or alcohol from the body of a chemically dependent person, with or without the use of other drugs.

dysfunctional: Impaired or abnormal functioning.

ethyl alcohol: The intoxicating agent in beer, wine, and liquors that is formed during the process of fermentation.

fetal alcohol syndrome: A condition in which unborn babies become damaged by excessive alcohol use by the mother; negative effects include damaged organs, birth defects, mental retardation, and learning disabilities.

genetic: Hereditary.

habitual: Something resorted to on a regular basis; a habit.

hallucination: An illusion of seeing or hearing something not actually present.

hangover: Disagreeable physical effects such as headache, nausea, and fatigue the day after excessive drinking.

hepatitis: A disease characterized by an inflamed liver, sometimes caused by prolonged heavy drinking.

hereditary: Physical traits or behaviors passed down in families through the genes.

illicit: Something illegal.

inhibition: The act of restraining one's behavior.

intoxication: Becoming drunk.

metabolism: The chemical and physical changes in living cells that involve maintenance of life.

minor: One who is under the legal drinking age, in most states age twenty-one.

miscarriage: The premature death of a fetus in the uterus.

neurochemical: Chemicals found in the nervous system (brain, spinal cord, etc.).

outpatient: A patient who visits a clinic or hospital but does not stay the night.

pancreatitis: Inflammation of the pancreas.

placenta: The vascular, membranous structure that supplies a fetus with nourishment before its birth.

precursor: That which precedes or indicates the approach of something else.

predisposition: Having a susceptibility for something; being more likely than others to develop a condition, such as a disease.

promiscuous: Having more than one sexual partner.

recoveree: An alcoholic or drug addict who is in recovery.

rehabilitation: Being in a state of recovery, as from an addiction.

relapse: The return of a person in a recovery program to drinking or drug taking.

REM sleep: The stage of sleep during which dreaming occurs.

sedative: Any type of drug that has a calming effect.

seizures: A sudden bodily attack, usually characterized by uncontrollable shaking.

sobriety: A state of mental clarity reached through abstinence from alcohol and other drugs; being "drug-free."

social drinking: Light drinking that does not result in intoxication.

sponsor: An individual in a twelve-step program who undertakes to guide and serve as mentor to another member.

sting operation: Undercover police operation.

tolerance: The need to consume an increased amount of alcohol in order to achieve the same intoxicating effects.

toxic: Poisonous.

tremor: Any continued and involuntary trembling of the body.

ulcer: An inflamed sore on a mucous membrane (like the stomach lining) that results in destruction of the tissue.

withdrawal: Physical and emotional symptoms that develop when an individual who is physically addicted to alcohol stops drinking, and levels of alcohol begin to drop in the body.

Organizations
to Contact

The following national organizations provide services or information about alcoholism treatment and support groups. Local phone books generally list service referral and hot-line numbers for these services in each state.

Al-Anon
PO Box 862, Midtown Station
New York, NY 10018
U.S. Meeting Information:
(800) 344-2666

Al-Anon support groups are made up of family and friends of alcoholics who meet to share their experiences and to solve common problems. Al-Anon is not affiliated with any religious denomination, political group, or other organization. Membership is free.

Alateen
PO Box 862, Midtown Station
New York, NY 10018
U.S. Meeting Information:
(800) 344-2666

An offshoot of Al-Anon, Alateen is a support group for teens who are not alcoholics themselves, but who worry about someone else's drinking, such as friends, siblings, or parents.

Alcoholics Anonymous (AA)
General Service Office
PO Box 459
Grand Central Station

New York, NY 10163
(212) 870-3400

One of the most widely adopted aftercare programs for alcoholics, Alcoholics Anonymous is a twelve-step mutual help program that stresses sobriety through spiritual growth.

Mothers Against Drunk Driving (MADD)
511 E. John Carpenter Freeway, Suite 700
Irving, TX 75062
(214) 744-6233
800-GET-MADD

There are more than six hundred chapters of Mothers Against Drunk Driving nationwide. Members in each chapter work to find solutions to the drunk driving problem and underage drinking. They are supportive of families who have lost loved ones due to drunk driving accidents.

National Clearinghouse for Alcohol and Drug Information (NCADI)
PO Box 2345
Rockville, MD 20847-2345
800-729-6686
800-487-4889 TDD (Hearing Impaired)
fax: (301) 468-6433
e-mail: info@health.org
Internet: http://www.health.org

An organization run by the federal government that provides free information (books, pamphlets, etc.) on substance abuse, including material about alcohol geared specifically for teens.

Students Against Drunk Driving (SADD)
PO Box 800
Marlboro, MA 01752
(508) 481-3568

SADD offers help to schools that want to set up their own chapters. It encourages peer counseling among students on saying no to drinking and drugs and aims to increase public awareness about drunk driving.

Suggestions for Further Reading

Claudia Black, *It Will Never Happen to Me*. New York: Random House, 1981.

Jane Claypool, *Alcohol and You*. New York: Franklin Watts, 1981.

Susan Cohen and Daniel Cohen, *A Six-Pack and a Fake ID: Teens Look at the Drinking Question*. New York: M. Evans, 1986.

Paul Dolmetsch, ed., *Teens Talk About Alcohol and Alcoholism*. Garden City, NY: Doubleday, 1987.

George B. Eager, *Peer Pressure*. Rev. ed. Valdosta, GA: Mailbox Club Books, 1993.

Alan Lang, *Alcohol: Teenage Drinking*. New York: Chelsea House, 1992.

Nancy J. Nielsen, *Teen Alcoholism*. San Diego: Lucent Books, 1990.

Elizabeth A. Ryan, *Straight Talk About Drugs and Alcohol*. Rev. ed. New York: Facts On File, 1995.

Roger E. Vogler, *Teenagers & Alcohol: When Saying No Isn't Enough*. Philadelphia: Charles Press, 1992.

Elen Wijnberg, *Alcohol*. Chatham, NJ: Raintree, 1993.

Works Consulted

Brian Akre, "New Program Tries to Scare Kids Away from Drugs, Alcohol, and Death," Associated Press, March 1997. Internet: http://ap611316.htm@smartwine.com

"Alcohol Alert," National Institute on Alcohol and Alcoholism No. PH 329, January 1993. Internet: http://www.niaaa.nih.gov

"Alcohol Alert," National Institute on Alcohol and Alcoholism No. PH 345, July 1993. Internet: http://www.niaaa.nih.gov

Jim Bernat, "My Boyfriend Was a Binge Drinker," *Teen Magazine*, December 1995.

Ed Carson, "Purging, Bingeing," *Reason*, December 1995.

R. Clapper, "A retrospective study of risk-taking and alcohol-mediated unprotected intercourse," *Journal of Substance Abuse*, no. 3, 1991.

Roy DeLaMar, "The Truth About Teens and Drugs: Why Just 'Just Say No' Hasn't Worked," *Family Circle*, March 12, 1996.

Sandra Eckstein, "House OKs Teen Driving, DUI Measure," *Atlanta Journal-Constitution*, March 1997. Access Atlanta, Internet: http://www.accessatlanta.com/ajc/

Ralph Ellis, "An empty Christmas: Kimberly Shaffer faces life without her three children and the father of her unborn child as the speeding teenager who hit them Wednesday remains: 'in disbelief,'" *Atlanta Journal and Constitution*, December 22, 1995.

———,"Coweta man gets 10 years for wreck that killed five: Sentence called too lenient by family members, MADD," *Atlanta Journal and Constitution*, July 26, 1996.

Sandy Fertman, "The Highs and Lows of Teen Drinking," *Teen Magazine*, March 1995.

Patricia Anne Goins, "The Role of Disinhibition in Adolescent Sexual Behavior: Assessment of Alcohol, Marijuana, and Tobacco Use." Master's thesis, San Diego State University, 1993.

Enoch Gordis, M.D., ed., *Eighth Special Report to the U.S. Congress on Alcohol and Health*. Alexandria, VA: Department of Health and Human Services, 1993.

Ben Gose, "The Party's Over," *Chronicle of Higher Education*, October 13, 1995.

Tony Guy, "Undercover Teen: Busting the Bad Guys," *Teen Magazine*, March 1996.

Wendy J. Hamilton, "Recognizing Adolescent Alcohol Abuse: A Family Guide," New Mexico State University, May 22, 1996. Internet: http://elroy.nmsu.edu/cahe/redtops/f-111.html

Hazelden Center, *A Guide for Teens* (booklet). Minnesota: Hazelden Foundation, 1994.

Roberta Israeloff, "Teaching Your Child About Drugs and Alcohol," *Parents Magazine*, October 1995.

Jean Kinney and Gwen Leaton, *Loosening the Grip*. St. Louis: Times Mirror, 1987.

MADD, "Public Policy," March 1997. Internet: http://www.policy@MADD.org

Matt McGue, "Parent and Sibling Influences on Adolescent Alcohol Use and Misuse," *Journal of Studies on Alcohol*, vol. 57, no. 1, January 1996.

Tara Meyer, "Fatal crashes involving teen drivers drop nationwide," *Seattle Times*, December 6, 1996.

J. R. Moehringer, "Why?" *Los Angeles Times*. Home edition, Los Angeles Times Magazine Section, July 28, 1996.

Julie Monahan, "True Stories: Teens with Drinking Problems," *Teen Magazine*, April 1993.

Judy Monroe, "Alcohol and Ads: What Effect Do They Have on You?" *Current Health 2*, vol. 21, no. 3, November 1994.

Al J. Mooney, Arlene Eisenberg, and Howard Eisenberg, *The Recovery Book*. New York: Workman, 1992.

F. Mott, "Linkages between sexual activity and alcohol and drug use among American adolescents," *Family Planning Perspectives*, no. 20, 1988.

Roberta Anne Myers, "Sobriety High," *Seventeen*, February 1995.

Bob Ortega, "Efforts to Reduce Teen Drinking May Provide Lessons," *Wall Street Journal*, August 19, 1995.

Evelyn Peterson, "Teenage Drinking and Driving," *Parent Talk Newsletter*, May 14, 1996. Internet: http://www.ParentsPlace.com

"Preventing Teenage Alcohol Use—It's EASY," *Addiction Letter*, June 1994.

Warren Richards, "I Drove Drunk," *Seventeen*, November 1993.

J. Max Robins, "Current Ads May Be Alcohol's Last Call," *TV Guide*, February 2–8, 1996.

J. Rolf, "Substance misuse and HIV & AIDS risks among delinquents: A prevention challenge," *International Journal of Addictions*, vol. 25, no. 4A, 1991.

Carol Silverman Saunders, "It's Suicide," *Current Health 2*, vol. 22, no. 6, February 1996.

Alvin Silverstein and Virginia B. Silverstein, *Alcoholism*. Philadelphia: Lippincott, 1975.

"The Fact Is," Join Together, March 1997. Internet: http://www.jointogether.org

Alexander C. Wagenaar, "Where and How Adolescents Obtain Alcoholic Beverages," *Public Health Reports*, vol. 108, no. 4, July/August 1993.

Fara Warner, "Liquor Industry Tackles Teenage Drinking," *Wall Street Journal*, June 30, 1995.

Pamela Warrick, "In an Instant . . . ," *Los Angeles Times*, November 1, 1995.

Drake Witham, "Recovery in the Dorm," *Chronicle of Higher Education*, November 10, 1995.

"Zero Tolerance," *New York Times*, June 11, 1995.

Index

About the Author

Hayley R. Mitchell holds a master of fine arts degree in poetry from the University of Washington and a master's degree in literature from California State University, Long Beach. Her award-winning poetry has been published in numerous literary journals throughout the United States, and she edits and publishes the small press poetry magazine *Sheila-Na-Gig*. She currently teaches composition and creative writing at various universities and community colleges in southern California.

Picture Credits

Cover photo: © Ron Chapple/FPG, Inc.
AP Photo/Al Behrman, 61
AP Photo/Beloit Daily News, Tom Holoubek, 76
AP Photo/Dan Hulshizer, 60
AP Photo/MADD, Tyler Mallory, 64
AP Photo/Toby Talbot, 23
AP Photo/Paul Vathis, 53, 55
AP/Wide World Photos, 31
© Biophoto Associates/SS, Photo Researchers, Inc., 19
Richard Gold, 17
© Evan Johnson, Impact Visuals, 73
© Catherine Karnow, Woodfin Camp & Associates, Inc., 13
© Lisa R. Kereszi, Impact Visuals, 47
© Andy Levin/Science Source, Photo Researchers, Inc., 21
© 1990 Andrew Lichtenstein, Impact Visuals, 67
© 1993 Andrew Lichtenstein, Impact Visuals, 8
© 1994 Andrew Lichtenstein, Impact Visuals, 26
© 1992 Piet van Lier, Impact Visuals, 50
© Brian Palmer, Impact Visuals, 34
© Stephanie Rausser, Impact Visuals, 14
Leif Skoogfors, Woodfin Camp & Associates, Inc., 75
Sobriety High School, 70
UPI/Corbis-Bettmann, 63
© Jim West, Impact Visuals, 41